OLD-TIME

RADIO

MEMORIES

by Mel Simons

Also by Mel Simons:

The Old-Time Radio Trivia Book

The Old-Time Television Trivia Book

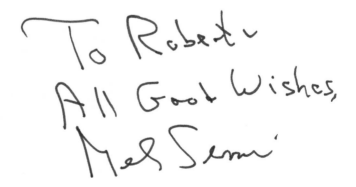

OLD-TIME RADIO MEMORIES

by Mel Simons

BearManor Media
2007

Old-Time Radio Memories

© 2007 Mel Simons

For information, address:

BearManor Media
P. O. Box 71426
Albany, GA   31708

bearmanormedia.com

Cover design by John Teehan

Typesetting and layout by John Teehan

Published in the USA by BearManor Media

ISBN—1-59393-078-X

Dedication

This book is dedicated to my late grandmother, Rae Slate, and my nephews, Michael Weinrauch and David Goldman

Mel Simons

Table of Contents

Foreword

Mel Simons has a great gift for digging up old scripts, old shows, and old actors. He has a typewriter, four shovels, and a backhoe. Nevertheless, they are most pleasant memories, very accurate and highly entertaining.

Mel's other books are equally interesting and deal with information from radio and television. If you want to be the best informed trivia person in your circle...get all the books, light some candles, and read to your utter enjoyment. That's what Ben Franklin did, and look where he wound up.

Enjoy this book. Mel Simons is a great writer and a very nice man, and I've always suspected him.

– Norm Crosby

The interviews contained in this book were conducted in person at an old-time radio convention at Dunfey's Resort on Cape Cod, or at WBZ Radio in Boston by telephone. They all took place in 1975.

Acknowledgements

I am most grateful to the people who made this book possible—the old-time radio performers who graciously agreed to be interviewed, and for the many hours of pleasure they gave me during the glory days of radio.

I would also like to thank four very special people:

Shelly Strickler, who writes the back covers of my books,
as well as my brochures

Kim Malo, a computer genius, who created my website

Bud Giordano, who fixes the many things I often break,
and is a great friend

Wayne Boenig, who helps me find many rare radio shows,
and is also a great friend

Edgar Bergen
The Charlie McCarthy Show

Mel   Mr. Bergen, I can't tell you what a pleasure it is to talk to you, sir.

E.B.   Well, that's very flattering.

Mel   There is no bigger Edgar Bergen fan in the world than myself. I kind of grew up with you. I never missed your Sunday night show at 8 o'clock.

E.B.   It started in 1937 and went on until 1957. That's a pretty long record.

Mel   Boy, it sure is. How did it all begin for you?

E.B.   Well, I played vaudeville for 10 years, until I killed it! I played all over America, Australia, England, and all that. Then vaudeville started dying out, so I was going to switch to nightclubs. I was booked into the Helen Morgan Club in New York.

I had the idea that it might be a good idea to do Esquire man. He was kind of a ladies' man, and a nightclub man, you know the blond mustached man on *Esquire Magazine*. They don't use him anymore. I asked permission, and they said yes. And then when I asked for written permission, a little later, I said I'm booked in the Helen Morgan Club, and they said they changed their mind.

Edgar Bergen and Charlie McCarthy

They would rather have known only in the magazine. That was the nicest thing they ever did to me, or else they would have owned Charlie McCarthy!

So I decided to put Charlie in top hat, monocle and tails, and we were the first ventriloquist act in nightclubs. These were always singers and dancers, up to that time.

Mel   Very interesting.

E.B.   Lunt and Fontanne were playing New York, and they would come in a couple times a week while I played the Helen Morgan Club. They were real fans.

Then I was booked into the Rainbow Room at Radio City, and Elsa Maxwell threw the four hundred party at The Waldorf, and Noel Coward was the guest of honor. She got the idea of hiring me and having Charlie heckle Noel, rather than flattering him. So we heckled him, and it went over very well.

As a successful party giver, Elsa got booked on the *Rudy Vallee Radio Show*. And they said to her, "How do you give successful parties? Why are you famous?" She said, "Well, here's my secret. I put all the dull people at the same table, and put all the brilliant ones at the same table. Then everybody is happy! Then I book a ventriloquist."

They said, "Who is the ventriloquist?" She said, "Edgar Bergen." They said, "Maybe we'll book him on the show."

So with apologies, they booked me on. And when the president of J. Walter Thompson heard they booked a ventriloquist on, he said, "Well he damn well better be funny. So that was the beginning of it, the *Rudy Vallee Show*.

I then played the Chez Paree in Chicago. And I went over to NBC and auditioned for a man there, Clarence Menzer, who was the head of the studio, and he said, "No, it will never go. They won't believe it, and the comedy isn't right. It's not funny!"

I said, "They're laughing at it at the Chez Paree." He said, "Radio is different." Well, he became vice president of NBC, and I became the biggest name they had on NBC.

Mel   You certainly did.

E.B.   So, you can make mistakes and still do all right.

Mel   Tell us about the *Rudy Vallee Show*.

E.B.   I was on the *Rudy Vallee Show* two or three times in December of 1936. Then they would pick up my option a week at a time. They did that for three weeks. They didn't think I could last longer than that. Then they got sold on me and said, "Let's round it out and make it 13 weeks by doing it 10 more."

Well, that was a big joy. Then I got panicky – where would I get all the material? You never know what you're capable of doing til you have a deadline.

So, then in May of '37, we opened the *Chase & Sanborn Show* out in Hollywood. So I moved out here.

Mel   When the *Chase & Sanborn Show* began in '37, did you have a cast of regulars?

E.B.   Yes, we began with Don Ameche, Dorothy Lamour, and Nelson Eddy. We had a guest star each week. We would pay $5,000 too. That's equivalent, with inflation, to about $15,000 today. And how many television shows will pay $15,000 for someone to come on and do six or seven minutes?

Mel   When was Mortimer Snerd introduced?

E.B.   He was introduced a good three or four years later, early '40s, '41 or so.

Mel   And how did he come to be?

E.B.   Well, he was really created before. When I was playing Chez Paree and the Waldorf, I would do so well I would bring out Charlie for encores. In bringing him out two or three times, I knew, was wrong from a vaudeville point of view. You should do something different, you know, a little different.

       So I had to have another dummy. So I checked over what voices I could produce. Something that wouldn't conflict with Charlie. A voice came up, a stupid voice, and that's how Mortimer developed.

       I drew on tablecloths, and studied character analysis, until I got a face that was a likeable, stupid-looking boy.

Mel   And the voice goes so perfectly with the character. You know, I own many of your old radio shows, and they are as funny now as when you did them. I'm always playing them for friends of mine.

Edgar Bergen and Charlie McCarthy

The shows you did with W.C. Fields, when did you get involved with him?

E.B.   Well, he was on the very first show, the *Chase & Sanborn Show*, in 1937. And then he was not on week after week, but on as often as we could get him, if his health would permit.

He sent me a fan letter when I went on the *Rudy Vallee Show*. He said, "What wonderful timing and comedy. Congratulations." He was in a sanitarium at the time.

Mel   Isn't that a nice thing to do.

E.B.   Yes, and so, when I got out there, why, we would naturally ask for him, and he came on. We never had the slightest disagreement. We admired each other, and I was so glad to have him, because he was so great to write for. And he was a good writer himself. We had some of the darndest lines. People thought he really hated kids and he hated Charlie. I read reviews that he did, and it's not true.

Mel   Not true at all?

E.B.   Not true. One day we were having a little writing session. He said, "I know Charlie likes me, because he always calls me "Mr. Fields." We, of course, we all treated Charlie as a human. I've a few celebrity stars that weren't going to play to a dummy and be taken in by it on the radio. They were going to be above it, and they got so screwed up! It's better to go along with the gag.

Mel   You know, I got the impression many times, listening to you with Fields, that many times a great deal of it was adlib and wasn't written.

E.B.   Oh yes, well, with Fields I would go to his house Monday morning. I would go with a script girl and another writer. We would talk and build up the next week's show. He would write jokes, and he would come up with ideas, and I would write jokes.

Then we would bring the final script to him and say, "Now, this is it, Bill." I said, "This is the way we're gonna do it." He said, "Yes, that's it." I said, "All right." So, of course, I knew he would dirty it up!

Don Ameche was very good at keeping it under control, and then we'd get so wild that the director then would come up and give us, you know, two minutes to get to the finish.

To me, Fields was by far my favorite guest. He could write. He could do comedy, he could do pantomime, and he could play what you wrote for him.

Mel   And I get the impression you generally liked him as a person.

E.B.   Oh yes, I did. I would go to his house for dinner. He would have dinners there with John Barrymore, Gene Fowler, and stag dinners of about eight or 10 people. You'd think it might be pretty wild and pretty stag, but it wasn't at all. It was a very intellectual, inspiring evening done in grand style. Flaming desserts like cherry jubilee.

And I just sat and listened. It was a great experience for me.

Mel   As you think back to your 20 years in radio, do you have any particular fond memories of the show?

E.B.   Well, yes, I made lifelong friendships. I celebrated my 70th birthday a year or two ago, and my wife planned it. A surprise party, a stag dinner. Some of the friends that were there were Ray Noble, Tony Stanford, the director, Joel Bigelow, a writer, Don Ameche, and a lot of the people with the show.

Mel   Who were some of your favorite guests, personally, off the top of your head?

E.B.   Well, Charles Laughton was another good one to fight with. He loved doing it too. He was such a touchy sort, easily hurt, you know, kind of a miserable character. He was sulking because Charlie always got under his skin.

One night I said to him, "Charlie wants to apologize for what he said last time." He said, "Well, that's very generous of Charlie."

And Charlie said, "I'll do more than that. I not only want to apologize for what I said last time, but for what I'm gonna say to you tonight!"

Then Charlie would say, "Is it true, Mr. Laughton, that you played the Hunchback of Notre Dame without any makeup?" A beautiful insult.

But the only difference, I would say, through the years, is today the insults hurt more. Today they have more bite to them.

Mel   In those days it was just a lot of fun. Any other favorite guests, besides W.C. Fields and Charles Laughton? Any others come to mind?

E.B.   Oh, there were many. Carole Lombard was charming, and we had lots of fun. She would rant and rave about being in love with Charlie. She once said to Charlie, "What happened to this undying love?" Charlie said, "I don't know. I guess it died!"

Anita Gordon was a singer on the show.

Mel   Yes, I remember.

E.B.   She was so good at lines. She never got flustered. We auditioned her during the war. Her agent said, "Would you just let her sing a song to audition?" And he said, "Because her father has a butcher shop. He's a meat cutter. If I can just get her an audition, I'm set for steaks! I'm set for meat!"

So we said, "Sure, we'll audition her." We auditioned her, and we liked her, and we hired her. And he said, "You don't have to hire her. You don't have to do it."

She went on our network show, the first time, 16 years old, and sang beautifully. As she sang, she touched the music stand on the first show, and it fell over, and her music was on it. She just reached down, kept singing, and picked up the music. Looked over at me, while singing, and winked at me! Now that's calmness, you know.

Mel   Did the Bickersons get their start with you?

E.B.   Well, yes, they did. That was their big thing, starting with us. I don't know if they had done anything before with it, but they were booked on as a team. They were Don Ameche and Frances Langford.

Mel   I was always under the impression that they began their career on your show.

E.B.   Of course, we had Mae West on too.

Mel   Tell me about Mae West.

E.B.   Well, it looked all right on paper. She can't even say hello without "C'mon up to my room." Everything she said had that sexy intonation. She once had a line, "Charlie, why don't you come up and see me sometime?"

        And Charlie said, "Well, I don't know. I'll have to think that over; it takes time."

        And she said, "I like a man who takes his time!"

        Well, the network apologized, the agency apologized, and I went out of town and hid! And the ratings went up two points!

Mel   Well, Mr. Bergen, I want to thank you very much for your time. I can't tell you what it has meant to me personally. You've always been one of my favorites.

E.B.   Well, I've been around quite a while now. I enjoyed talking to you. Good-bye.

Ezra Stone
The Aldrich Family

Mel   I grew up with Henry Aldrich as a kid. I never missed you. You were on every Thursday night.

E.S.   That's right, mostly Thursdays.

Mel   May I ask you, how did it all begin for you?

E.S.   *The Aldrich Family?*

Mel   Yes.

E.S.   I created the part of Henry Aldrich in a play called *What a Life* by Clifford Goldsmith. It was produced by George Abbott. It was around 1939…no, '38, I guess. My memory for dates is pretty bad, but you can look it up.

Mel   I certainly will. This was done on Broadway?

E.S.   Right.

Mel   Had you done any radio work up until this?

Best to regards
to Mel Simons.
I certainly don't
look like this now
and doubt that
I ever did.
Sincerely,
Ezra Stone "Henry Aldrich" 6/7/75

Ezra Stone as Henry Aldrich

E.S.   Yes, I was a kid actor in Philadelphia on the *Horn and Hardart Children's Hour.*

Mel   How did Henry Aldrich get his start on radio, after the Broadway success?

E.S.   Rudy Vallee had a policy on his *Fleischmann's Yeast Hour* of doing scenes from current Broadway productions. We did a scene from the play on the *Rudy Vallee Show*, July, I believe, of our first year.

The producers, J. Walter Thompson, Standard Brands, asked Mr. Goldsmith to come back for two more appearances, in specially written material, using the same characters. And we did. That was in the days of Joe Penner and Charlie McCarthy and Abbott and Costello. They were all starting out on radio as individual acts, which was long before any of them had their own shows. The

Rudy Vallee Show was kind of the *Ed Sullivan Show* of its day.

Rudy presented variety performers on radio in debut performances. Then he would bring them back as the audience reaction seemed to work.

In competition with Rudy Vallee in that same era was Kate Smith. By competition I mean she also had a variety show, and they competed for the same talent. Major guest stars and up-and-coming acts. Kate Smith was under contract to General Foods, and they were direct competitors to Standard Brands. They bid for our services and bid the most. So after three appearances on the *Rudy Vallee Show*, we then were signed to do 39 on the *Kate Smith Hour*, in an eight-minute sketch.

After those 39 weeks, we were then signed to a contract by General Foods for us to go on our own time for a half hour. We began as a summer replacement for Jack Benny. After that one summer replacing Jack Benny we then went on our own time. We were on for 15 years.

Mel   I think you were one of the top-rated programs.

E.S.   Not really! Only in the summer, when the other big shows went off the air, did we make the top 10. We were in about the top 20, 15 or 20.

Mel   As you think back, do you have any particular fond memories of the show? Anything that sticks out in your mind?

E.S.   Well, not really. It only consumed nine hours a week of my time, and I was so involved in other activities, as a director, that it was certainly not my major responsibility. I don't put it down, and I enjoyed it, but I had many more challenges the rest of my working week. I was both a director and a teacher.

Mel   What were you teaching then?

E.S.   I had been teaching acting ever since I graduated from the American Academy of Dramatic Arts in 1935. At the same time, I was raising a family. We had a home on a working dairy farm in Pennsylvania. So I had plenty of pleasurable activities around me.

Mel   What were you directing in those days?

E.S.   Well, my first Broadway credit starred Milton Berle in a play called *See My Lawyer*.

Mel   What else did you direct?

E.S.   *This Is the Army, Me and Molly, Reunion in New York.*

Mel   How about your present activities? What are you working on now?

E.S.   Well, I'm a freelance television and film director. I just completed a bicentennial documentary on immigration called *The Forty Million*. Lorne Greene does the narration. And I'm very active. I'm on a retainer with IBM as a general director and consultant on their recognition events and audio visuals for their general systems division.

I'm vice chairman of the board of the American National Theater and Academy. I'm involved with the American College Theater Festival.

Mel   What do you do in your spare time?

E.S.   [Laughs] I also do workshops around the world for Army Special Services.

Mel   Do you ever get out to the East? Do you ever get out to Boston?

E.S.   I haven't been to Boston in some time.

Mel   I want to thank you very much for your time.

E.S.   Not at all.

Mel   It was a great pleasure talking to you.

E.S.   Thank you very much.

Lon Clark

Nick Carter, Master Detective

Mel   First of all, Lou, Sunday evenings, between you and *The Shadow*, was the greatest evening of the week for me growing up.

L.C.   Well, that's nice to hear.

Mel   I would never miss *Nick Carter, Master Detective*. I loved the show, and you were the only person to play Nick Carter.

L.C.   Yes, I created the role and played it for over 12 years.

Mel   Can you tell me, basically, how it started? How you happened to begin doing Nick Carter?

L.C.   Well, WOR radio in New York got the rights to the show from the magazine publishing company. The way they did it in those days was they would call in what they felt were suitable performers that might be likeable and proper for the roles.

We came in, and we auditioned, just like today, they screen-test people for various film roles. Then they have a committee that sits down and listens to all the different voices that have been recorded and the lucky man gets the nod. It was a very pleasing thing to me to have the director of the show call me up one

Lon Clark and Bret Morrison

evening and say, "Lon, we're unanimous in our decision that we'd like to have you do the role if you're interested. Come on in and talk contracts." And that's the way it began.

Mel   What were the years you were on?

L.C.   I'm a little hazy. I'm probably off by a year or so. But I think that we went on the air around 1945, and I think that we went off the air about 12 to 13 years later.

Mel   Prior to doing *Nick Carter*, were you on radio?

L.C.   Oh, yes indeed.

Mel   Can you kind of fill me in?

L.C.   Yes, I was one of the crew of New York radio performers. I worked practically all of the shows that were in New York, at one time or another. I used to do as many as 20 broadcasts a week. And that's a lot of shows. And it made for a very, very long day.

I'd be in the studio sometimes in the morning at 6:30 rehearsing, and might not get home until around 1 o'clock in the morning. In those early days of radio, they didn't have tape. So, if you had

Lon Clark

a show that was being played in New York, let's say Manhattan at midnight, and it went on the air at 8:30 to 9:00 in New York, that same show would be repeated from 11:30 to 12:00, to be played for the West Coast, because of the three hours difference in time. So that meant that we had some very, very long days.

We had rehearsals, then you dress, then your air time. And so, how do you figure you get 22 shows in? Some of them were 15-minute shows, with an hour-and-a-half rehearsal. Other shows would be a half-hour show that you do at night, with probably four to five hours rehearsal.

So very often, if the directors of these shows wanted you specifically, they might even say to you, "Look, if you can't make the full rehearsal time, I still want you on the show," and they would let you come in when you could. I ran from one show to another. I can tell you, I drank an awful lot of coffee out of paper cups over the years. I hate to look at a paper cup today!

Mel   What were some of the shows you were on?

L.C.   Oh, I did quite a few of the soap operas. *Bright Horizon* was one of them. I used to be the announcer on *The Kate Smith Hour*. I was the announcer on *Plantation Party*. I was on *The March of Time*. On Saturday mornings I would be doing *Report to the Nation*. I did *Bulldog Drummond*, *The Thin Man*.

You know, the beautiful thing about radio is this – because you were behind the microphone, the public didn't see who you were. If you were a versatile person, gifted in changing your voice, people would decide what you looked like, according to how your voice sounded.

Mel   Was *Nick Carter* a fun show for you to do, Lon?

L.C.   Oh yes, it always was. It was fun to a great degree, but when you play the same role for 12 years, and you're conscientious about sounding as though it's the first time that you're ever heard in that role, you didn't want to sound bored. Because so many lines reappear week in and week out, and week in and week out. To make lines sound as though you're saying them for the first time required a great deal of effort on your part. You had to be on your toes.

Mel   I can well imagine.

L.C.   You know, I know actors who played roles for a long period of time and suddenly then become glib. They aren't thinking. The lines come so easy that there is no real creation behind saying it as though you're saying it for the first time. I always wanted to sound like I was deeply interested in what I'm doing. I maintain that if an actor doesn't sound like he cares, how do you expect the audience to care?

Mel   As you think back, Lon, do you have any particular fond memories, or perhaps humorous things that happened?

L.C.   I will tell you one story that really is a delightful one. Toward the end of the days of radio, when television was taking over, the advertising agencies began to neglect radio. They felt radio was now going to die away slowly. So radio show after radio show was going off the air. *Nick Carter* was one of the very last detective shows to go off the air, if not the last one.

One night, toward the end of our term, somebody pushed the wrong button at WOR. Just at the end of the show, the announcer said, "And now back to the conclusion of our Nick Carter story for today," and Patsy said, "Nick, how did you ever determine the fact that so and so was the killer?" And I said, "Patsy, it was obvious." And at that moment, the engineer cut in another show. So nobody heard the end of the show. WOR switchboards were lighted up for two hours. They had hundreds and hundreds of calls coming in. As a result of it, the newspapers got the story, and the next day on *The New York Times*, *The New York Post*, and *The Daily News* there were headlines: "Is Radio Dead? Not If You Were Listening to Nick Carter!"

Mel   When did the show go off?

L.C.   I think around 1955, something like that. I think the principal reason why radio drama finally came to almost a total end, was the fact that the advertising agencies and the networks began to go to TV, and that was it for radio.

Mel   Thank you very much for a super interview.

Bret Morrison
The Shadow

Mel   Brett, my greatest punishment as a kid was when I would do something wrong and my folks wouldn't let me listen to *The Shadow*. How did it all begin for you?

B.M.   Well, I had just gotten out of Special Services in the Army, and I came to New York in 1943. I had been in Chicago up to that time. I had done radio out here on the West Coast, and I had done radio in Chicago. But I had not been to New York. So this was my first New York venture.

I was stationed in Boston. So that when I was through and mustered out I naturally headed for New York. I started to work almost immediately in radio. In a matter of a couple of weeks I had all the work I could handle.

I got a call for an audition one day. I was on the air until a quarter of the hour, and at the audition they were losing the studio on the hour. I didn't know what it was for. The audition was for 2 o'clock, and I said, "Well, I'm on the air til a quarter of 2. I'm not quite sure I can make it. I have to go cross town." And in New York, most of it has to be done on foot because of the traffic problem or one thing or another. So they said, "Well, do the best you can anyway."

So I got there like two minutes before the hour. They said, "Well, we're sorry, but we are losing the studio at 2 o'clock. Here, take this and just go in and read the opening and closing in your own way."

Bret Morrison as The Shadow

I did, and it was the opening and closing of *The Shadow*. It was the signature of *The Shadow*. I was Mr. First Nighter, you know, before that. And we used to follow *The Shadow*. So I would always hear the closing signature. So I just read it sort of the way I always heard it. I figured that's the end of that.

A couple of weeks later, I got a call saying, "You're it!" So that was it. The year was 1944.

Mel   1944, and the series went til when?

B.M.   1956.

Mel   1956, wow! You are the person most people associate with that role, even though there were a couple of other gentlemen that played the role before you.

B.M.   Yes, there were two others that played the role before me. They both did it very briefly.

Mel   Very, very briefly. Now, was Grace Matthews Margo all those years?

B.M.   No, the first Margo I worked with was Marjorie Anderson. And then Lesley Woods did it for a while, and then Grace Matthews, and then Gertrude Warner.

Mel   How many years was Grace with you?

B.M.   I don't remember offhand.

Mel   Isn't it funny? That's the Margo that I associate with as I was growing up.

B.M.   Yeah, I think she did it for several years. Gertrude came in later on, sort of after we went to tape, in the '50s

Mel   Was it a fun show for you to do?

B.M.   Yes, it was. When we first did it, you know, we did it live at the Long Acres Theatre.

Mel   In New York?

B.M.   Yes, in New York, with an audience. It was kind of fun, Sundays at 5 o'clock New York time. I was referred to as "the 5 o'clock Shadow"! It was fun. It was interesting. Of course, it was just one of the many shows that I did during that time.

Mel   How long were you Mr. First Nighter?

B.M.   Well, I was Mr. First Nighter from about 1937 or '38. I came back to Chicago from the coast in '37. So it must have been like around late '37 or early '38, until the war, around '42, so it was about four years or so.

Mel   What other shows were you associated with besides *The Shadow* and *First Nighter*?

B.M.   Well, those were the two that I was most closely identified with. There were a lot of shows that I did, especially out here, in the early '30s. I remember doing *Lux Radio Theater*, *Camel Caravan*, and things of that kind, a lot of the big shows. Those shows came from the coast in the early '30s.

Mel   Do you have any particular fond memories as you look back on your years with *The Shadow*?

B.M.   No, not really.

Mel   How about interesting anecdotes, maybe mistakes that happened, like gun shots that didn't work?

B.M.   Well, occasionally there might have been a gun shot that didn't go off, you know, but for the most part everyone was very professional. We were well-rehearsed. There really was never anything

Bret Morrison

that I can recall. As a matter of fact, in my entire career – except in the very early '30s, when we used to record like until 3 or 4 o'clock in the morning, on acetate in those days, if you made a mistake, you had to start at the top and go through it again – I can't recall a single incident of anything happening on a show that I was on. Maybe a gun not going off, and somebody adlibbing, you know, stabbed him instead of shooting him! Something of that kind.

Mel   Had you always wanted to go into broadcasting? Did you do
         anything prior to your radio career?

B.M.   I was always interested in the theater. I started when I was in
         school, as far as actual theater was concerned. I worked in a local
         stock company in Chicago. I did my first broadcast about 1928.
         The first thing I ever did on the air was the complete story of
         Dracula as a promotional series for Universal Pictures.

Mel   Was this done in Chicago?

B.M.   Yes, on WCSL, the voice of labor. I produced it, I directed it, I
         played the lead. I used such people as Hugh Marlowe, who at
         that time was a member of our theater group, and several people
         who later on became quite well known in the theater and in the
         movies.

         This was my introduction to radio. I had never been in front of
         a microphone before. As a result of this thing, I got a letter of
         introduction to Carl Everett Jr. out here. I came out here, to
         the coast, in the early '30s. I went to the Pasadena Playhouse,
         and I started doing main stage productions out there. They came
         out to the Playhouse looking for talent to do auditions for a
         radio show.

         I won the audition and did a show for Gilmore Gasoline, called
         Red Lion Trails. Hanley Stafford, who did Baby Snooks, was the
         announcer for the show. He was impressed with my work at the
         time. He recommended me to a couple of the directors out here
         who were doing radio.

         All of a sudden I started doing radio. Pretty soon that's all I was
         doing. Occasionally I would do a movie, but primarily radio. I
         started doing all the shows that came out of the West Coast.

         In 1937 I went back to Chicago to do the first singing-acting
         strip show on the air. It was called *Love Song*. It didn't last very
         long as a musical-drama thing, and finally evolved as a poetry-
         singing thing. And that was on for quite a while, and then *First*

Nighter and *The Chicago Theater of the Air*, and a lot of those shows that came out of Chicago at that time. Strip shows were there. *Helen Trent* used to be done there.

Mel   Interestingly, I met and spoke with Helen Trent this past Tuesday. She's living on Cape Cod, Julie Stevens, and she's a lovely gal. And I had an interview with her.

B.M.   When I did Helen, of course, it was done from Chicago, and Julie wasn't doing it. Someone else. I can't remember who.

Mel   It's interesting – if you were to meet people on the street and ask them to name their favorite radio shows, their top five, invariably, *The Shadow* is always named. It's a delight to talk to you.

B.M.   Thank you.

Rudy Vallee
The Rudy Vallee Show

Mel   Mr. Vallee?

R.V.   Yup.

Mel   How are you, sir?

R.V.   Who is this?

Mel   My name is Mel Simons, and I'm calling you from Boston, Mass.

R.V.   Yes.

Mel   I'm on a television station, WNAC-TV. I appear once a week and I talk about old-time radio.

R.V.   I'm not in the least bit interested in talking about it.

Mel   Well, actually, that leads to my next question. I'm writing a book on old-time radio, and how can I do a book without a bit on Rudy Vallee?

To Mel Simons

Rudy Vallee

R.V.   Well, you don't need me for that. Just write about it.

Mel   Well, could you fill in a few questions for me?

R.V.   What?

Mel   Could you fill in a few answers, I should say? I'd be most grateful to you, Mr. Vallee.

R.V.   Well, go ahead.

Mel   I'd like to ask you how it all began on radio for you.

R.V.   We started broadcasting from the Hi Ho Club at 35 East 53rd Street in New York City, in February of 1928. I had never heard an American radio program, and I decided to do some things that I had wanted to do all my life, in the way of changing keys, the selection of numbers, and we didn't have any brass section, so we couldn't play the stock orchestrations that every other band was playing.

         We only played choruses of songs. Why don't you go to the library and get a copy of my book, *Vagabond Dreams Come True*, and it will give you all the answers you want to know.

Mel   Oh, I sure will.

R.V.   Much more than I can give on the telephone, at the cost of the telephone wire. Just get the book *Vagabond Dreams Come True*. It will give you everything about the way we started and why.

Mel   There were a couple of other things I wanted to ask you in regard to people that you started. You started many, many entertainers.

R.V.   J. Walter Thompson agency and I chose a lot of performers for the *Fleischmann Hour*. They chose a lot of them; I chose a lot of them.

Mel   Who were some of the major artists that you chose?

R.V.   Everybody but Jack Benny. I usually didn't use him.

Mel   How about unknowns that you gave their start to on your program?

R.V.   We found a lot of persons who had been in vaudeville, but I took a lot of persons who had never done anything, because I thought they had something.

Mel   Could you give me a few names?

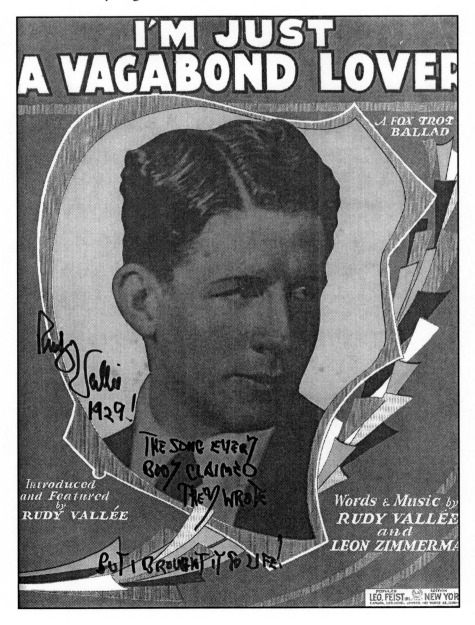

R.V.   No.

Mel   Til when was *Fleischmann's Yeast Hour* on?

R.V.   October 1929 to October 1939.

Mel   You were constantly in the top 10?

R.V.   We were probably the number-one variety show from 1932 to 1939.

Mel   You know, I spoke to Ezra Stone about 20 minutes ago, and he called you the Ed Sullivan of radio.

R.V.   No question about that.

Mel   Absolutely! And he told me how you gave him his start.

R.V.   Yes. I had nothing to do with his start. It was J. Walter Thompson. I merely presented him, but I didn't find him. I didn't even know he existed.

Mel   Are there any particular fond memories that you personally have of your radio show?

R.V.   No, you get these two books: *My Time Is Your Time* and *Vagabond Dreams Come True*. They'll give you all the details you need to know.

Mel   Well, Mr. Vallee, I thank you very much for you time. I certainly appreciate it.

R.V.   You're very welcome. Good-bye.

Julie Stevens
The Romance of Helen Trent

Mel   I'm sitting here with Julie Stevens from the most famous soap opera of all time, *The Romance of Helen Trent*. Julie, I want you to take me back to the beginning. How it all began with *Helen Trent*, how you started with it?

J.S.   Well, first of all, I was mainly interested in being in theater. And, therefore, New York was, at the time that I started in the business, the mecca for theater, as it still is. So I came to New York, and in order to eat while I was looking for that great break on Broadway, I was armed with a lot of letters to various people in the radio business.

I got some nice little jobs in radio. I was enjoying it, but still, the only thing that really interested me was theater. But I was working, and it was very nice. I proceeded to get a play. It was called *Brooklyn, U.S.A.*

In this play, *Brooklyn, U.S.A.*, a lot of the actors were radio people, and I mean important radio people. So they invited all the various directors and sponsors to come and see the opening night. So I was seen, along with the people who had sent for the sponsors. One person in particular decided that I would be right for the part of Kitty Foyle, which was then being cast. The director of the show said, "No, I don't think she'd be right," because I was playing a girl from Brooklyn, a rather low type. I had a Brooklyn accent, and the director kept saying, "No, she wouldn't be right."

And this casting director, Wilda Hinkel, kept saying, "Yes, I think Julie would be perfect." Well, they auditioned everybody, all the

37

Julie Stevens

radio people in New York. Now I had done, as I say, some radio parts but just small things here and there.

So I wasn't known at all, as far as radio was concerned, except for this play. They tested all the radio people. They still hadn't found the right person. So Miss Hinkel said, "Will you please call Julie Stevens, will you please? Just get her up here and listen to her."

Well, I arrived for the audition. I thought, now let's see, they saw me in the play, and to me it doesn't seem right that the part of Kitty Foyle should have a Brooklyn accent. But that's what they saw me in, so that must be what they want.

So I proceeded to audition for the part of Kitty Foyle with this Brooklyn accent, and this very strange kind of little character that I was playing. Well, of course, it was absolutely wrong. Miss Hinkel came out, and she said, "No, Julie," she said, "you just talk to us in your own voice."

Well, to make a long story short, I became Kitty Foyle. And for two years I very happily played the part. Bud Collyer was my leading man, and we had a wonderful time. It was a beautiful show. Carl Bixby wrote it, and it was beautifully written and directed. It was just a wonderful thing to be doing.

I was exclusively on that show for daytime, so I couldn't do any other daytime radio. I still, of course, was looking for a theater. But through that show, I began to really realize how lovely radio could be, and that it could do artistic, interesting things.

At that time, a lot of Chicago radio shows were coming to New York. Some of the casts were coming with the shows, and some of them were not. The woman who was playing Helen Trent was married and had a family, and they had a life in Chicago, and she couldn't move.

Mel   What was her name, Julie?

J.S.   Her name was Virginia Clark. So I had been called to audition for the part of Helen Trent. Well, I got the part, and for 16 years I was Helen Trent.

Mel   Sixteen years, til 1960, and so you went on in 1944?

J.S.   We went on in June of 1944, and we went off the air in June of 1960.

Mel   When did Helen begin, prior to you joining the show?

J.S.   I don't know, you see, because radio had never been any particular part of my life. I was strictly theater. That's all I cared about.

Mel   Now, while you were playing Helen Trent, did you play in any other shows?

J.S.   Yes, I did *Stella Dallas*, *Philip Morris Playhouse*, and *Abie's Irish Rose*.

Mel   Where were you born?

J.S.   I was born in St. Louis, and we spent our summers in Provincetown on Cape Cod. From my earliest recollection, I always wanted to be an actress.

Mel   As you think back, do you have any particular fond memories of *Helen Trent* or of radio in general?

J.S.   I remember Mary Jane Higby, who's a great, great friend of mine, who was the worst enemy that Helen Trent ever had on the show.

Mel   She played who on the show?

J.S.   She was Cynthia Swanson, my nemesis. She was the only one who took Gil Whitney away from me.

Mel   Who played your best friend, Agatha Anthony?

J.S.   Bess McCammon. She came on from Chicago and played the part.

Mel   And what about Gil Whitney? Who played him?

J.S.   Gil Whitney was David Gothard, and he had been Gil Whitney in Chicago.

Mel   So he was Gil Whitney throughout the run?

J.S.   As far as I know, he was always.

Mel   Do you ever hear from him?

J.S.   Yes, I do. He's very ill unfortunately in Los Angeles. I talked to him at Christmas.

Mel   It must have been a very sad day when *Helen Trent* left the air.

J.S.   No, no, actually it really wasn't. First of all, by that time, almost all of the soap operas had gone. I think I was about the last. *Our Gal Sunday* may have been very end one, but I was almost the last one to go.

Mel   I would venture to say that most people would say that *Helen Trent* was the most popular soap opera on radio.

J.S.   Well, that makes me very happy.

Mel   How did the name soap opera come to be?

J.S.   Well, that came to be because, I think, Procter & Gamble were the first sponsors of the daytime serials.

Mel   Who were a soap company?

J.S.   Yes.

Mel   I also would like to ask you about Lorelei Kilbourne.

J.S.   Oh well, I had decided that I wanted to try television. Just for my own satisfaction, to see if I could do it. I was asked to audition for *Big Town*. My husband was then director of programming at CBS, and CBS was doing *Big Town*. I had to turn down the audition, because he just didn't approve of that kind of family thing. So I didn't do that audition.

         Then my husband left CBS and went to ABC, and Mary Kay Wells, who played Lorelei, who was a friend of mine, was going to leave *Big Town*. She was going to get married.

Mel   What year was this?

J.S.   It was June of '59. Everything happens to me in June! So I got called and wound up playing Lorelei. I thoroughly enjoyed it. I had a very good time. And I was still doing *Helen Trent*.

         After a season and a half, the show moved to the West Coast, but I decided to stay in New York.

Mel   What are your present day activities? Tell us where you are living and what you are doing.

J.S.   I am living in a darling town on Cape Cod called Wellfleet. I am very happy there. My husband is retired, and we have a boat, and we absolutely love it. We have a greenhouse, and we do a lot of gardening.

         I also work for Ted Bell at his radio station called WVLC. We do *The Ted and Julie Show*, and it's a big hit.

Mel   Tell me about the show.

J.S.   We talk about theater, and we talk about films, and we talk about anything involving entertainment. It's an hour show, and we're on Wednesday mornings from 11 to noon.

Mel   Well, I want to thank you very much.

J.S.   Well, you're very welcome. Thank you, Mel.

Dennis Day

The Jack Benny Show,
A Day In the Life of Dennis Day

Mel   I am very happy to be here with Dennis Day. Dennis, I guess everybody kind of associates you with *The Jack Benny Show*. How did it all begin for you?

D.D.   Well, it started back in August of 1939. I sent a couple of recordings over to Jack Benny's agent, and Mary Livingstone one day came in and was listening to a lot of recordings of singers who were auditioning.

She liked my recording. She brought it to Chicago, to Jack. He came in and auditioned me. Then they gave me a round-trip ticket to go out to California to audition for his writers and producers, which I did.

And then, about three weeks before the show went on the air, I was signed to a contract, and I was with Jack all through those years, outside of my service in the Navy in World War II.

Mel   How many years were you with *The Benny Show*?

D.D.   Well, I was actually on the regular *Benny Show* 25 years. And I was associated with Jack for 35 years. In other words, I did his specials with him whenever he would do any specials. So my association with him goes back 35 years.

Mel   As you think back, Dennis, are there any particular fond memories, or perhaps some interesting anecdotes, that you could relate about Jack?

D.D.   Well, I have a lot of fond memories. One recent memory was just a year ago. My daughter was married, and we had a reception at my home. I sent Jack an invitation. He did come. Jack was so thoughtful. He called me up and said, "I will be there."

He came out and spent about two or three hours at the reception, visiting with everyone and with my daughter and her new husband. So it was a great thrill for me to have him there. It was the last time I saw Jack alive.

Mel   What are your personal thoughts on Jack Benny, the man? I'm sure you've been asked this dozens and dozens of times. But I'd still love to hear your take.

D.D.   Well, my personal feeling was that Jack was like a father to me. He gave me my break in show business. We had a special rapport between us. There was a genuine feeling of love, I think, he for me, and I certainly had it for him. This man was a very warm and very humble individual. Jack could be at a party, or be at a gathering, and he'd be sitting in a corner. He wouldn't be bothering with anybody. He wasn't the stereotype thought that people have of comedians, who are always cracking jokes and everything else. He was a wonderful individual. He loved family. He loved people.

Because of Jack, my wife and I have 10 children. We've got six at home. I've got four married. And he made all of this possible. So I have very warm, warm feelings for Jack. I have many great memories of this wonderful man.

Mel   Very, very nicely said. Let me ask you one last question, Dennis. Any humorous anecdotes that you can perhaps recall over the years, or funny things that happened on the show?

D.D.   Well, I remember going out with Jack. We had a break during rehearsal. We went across the street to get a cup of coffee. Jack wanted to make a phone call. So he made his call, and the operator said, "That'll be 10 cents." Well, he didn't have a dime, and he was the type of man, he didn't want to ask anyone.

So he said, "Well, operator, all I have is 25 cents."

She said, "Well, we'd be very happy to refund the change. What is your name, please?"

He said, "Operator, I know you won't believe this, but my name is Jack Benny!"

And of course, the operator said, "C'mon now, stop pulling my leg."

He said, "No, really, my name is Jack Benny," and kept insisting, "Well, please, if that's the way you're gonna carry on ...."

He said, "Oh, operator, please forget the whole thing. Forget I ever bothered you." And he hung up!

Because Jack had always, you know, with the image that he had, people always expected him to give a dime tip.

Mel   He was just the opposite, wasn't he?

D.D.   He was just the opposite. Even though it killed him, he had to overtip. I remember he did it to a cab driver. The meter only read about a dollar, and he gave him a buck and a half tip. The cab driver said, "No, please, Mr. Benny, you gotta take it back, because I don't want to destroy your image!"

Oh, he was such a great guy, though.

Mel   Well, I want to thank you very much. It's been a pleasure to meet you personally. I've been a fan for so many years.

D.D.   Thank you.

Don Wilson

Announcer on The Jack Benny Show

Mel   I am sitting here, at Dunfey's Hyannis Resort, with I would say, without fear of contradiction, my favorite announcer, my very favorite announcer...

D.W.   You say that about all the announcers!

Mel   I absolutely do not, Don Wilson. Don, my greatest memory of you is *The Jack Benny Show*. Let's go back before then, and may I ask you how and when your career on radio started?

D.W.   Well, my career on radio started about 1922 to '23 in the embryonic days before there was such a thing as commercial radio. In those days we had, as a receiver, we had a cat's whisker and a set of earphones with a coil of wire around an oatmeal box. That was your receiver. If you heard a transmitter six blocks down the street, you were home free. That was a great accomplishment.

Well, those were the early, early days, when radio was just cracking its shell. It progressed on to become the great attraction it was. Then you go into the '30s and '40s, and then things really began to pop wide open. Radio was the primary source of entertainment and information for practically the majority of Americans, I think, in those days. It took hold like wildfire and exploded into an electronic attraction that is only superseded by the TV monster that we have on our hands today.

Dennis Day and Don Wilson

It was a great privilege to be able to grow up through the industry. At the time that I started, I was in Denver, Colorado. Then I migrated to California, first to San Francisco, and then down to Los Angeles.

About 1928 I became associated with KFI in Los Angeles, the NBC flag station on the coast. It was independently owned but was the NBC outlet down there. I became chief of staff at KFI. My principal work, when I sort of got my feet on the ground, was doing sports. I played football through high school and college, and had a smattering of knowledge and a great enthusiasm for the sport.

So I talked the management into letting me do the broadcast of the Pacific Coast, NBC network football games. It was the Pacific Coast Conference. And that I did, beginning in 1928. In 1929 I did color on the Rose Bowl. Graham McNamee, one of the most beloved and revered names in all of radio, was the sportscaster for NBC at that time. He came out to the coast to do the

Rose Bowl. I worked with Mac as the color man. He did the play-by-play. In 1930, '31, '32, and '33 I was the play-by-play reporter. Mac no longer came out to the coast.

It was during that tenure of those years in the NBC Network, from the Rose Bowl, that NBC was prompted to invite me to join their staff in New York as a sports announcer. I went to New York as a sports announcer in the fall of 1933.

In the spring in 1934, I was thrown into a general audition with all the available staff boys at NBC and the freelance men around town to audition for a comedy show. I was the freshman, as far as time of service in New York for the network was concerned. I auditioned right along with the rest of them. It was for an announcer for *The Jack Benny Show*. Jack was changing clients from Chevrolet Motors to General Tires for the 13-week period to fill out that season.

I just got lucky. It sounds somewhat like a cop-out, my answer. But it isn't, because it's just exactly the way it happened. I read a few pages of script with Jack's writer while Jack listened in the booth. Jack came out; I read a few pages of script with him while the writer listened. I got lucky, and I got the job. It was the greatest day that ever happened to me in my life. That was the beginning of a 35-year period of association with Jack Benny. He was the greatest man in the business, beyond any question of doubt, in more ways than one. That was my lucky start. That's the way it all happened.

Mel   You know, one of the most thrilling experiences I ever had, Don, was last August to meet Jack Benny personally and sit and talk with him. I've always loved Jack Benny as a comedian, but Jack Benny, the person, seemed to me just like the person next door.

D.W.   Well, you struck on the key. Everyone knows Jack Benny for the great comedian and the great artist and performer that he was. But the key to Jack Benny is Jack Benny the man. Jack had so many great attributes of character. He was kind, tolerant, thoughtful, considerate, and above all, generous.

Now he has the reputation, of course, of being stingy. That was developed purely for the sake of his air character, and for laughs. Anybody that analyzes it sanely is very well aware of that. But as an example of Jack's generosity, let me cite to you that whenever Mrs. Wilson, who was professionally known as Lois Corbett, was playing stock, Jack was always at opening night. It didn't make any difference where she was playing. Now this is a typical example of Jack's generosity, in the giving of himself to encourage the people that were near to him on the air show, and help in any way that he could. The mere fact that he was present was a morale boost the likes of which you can't get any other way.

Jack was always that way with many of the people that were permanently associated with him on the show. Mary, Phil Harris, Dennis Day, Rochester, Mel Blanc, Frank Nelson. Jack was constantly doing things for people on the show.

You may recall the structure of *The Benny Show* from the early days on radio. Jack was frequently the butt end of the jokes. He was the man that the jokes bounced off of. He was a straight man more than he was a comedian. The supporting cast members had the laugh lines very, very frequently. This was contrary to any other comic that I know in the business that would dare do such a thing like that.

There was one time, way back in the early days of radio, we were on the air for 25 minutes out of 30 minutes before Jack ever got on microphone. He didn't say one word. We talked about him. He sat over on the other side of the stage. He mugged it, he got the laughs, he helped milk the laughs. But those of us that were in the supporting cast were the ones with the jokes. But the jokes all bounced off him. I don't know of any other comedian that has ever done anything like that. It was a courageous thing to do.

But this is a typical example, again, of Jack's generosity. He was that way all through the years. He was constantly doing whatever he could to build up the people that were associated with him on the show. His philosophy was very sound, very elementary. He knew that the bigger he could make the characters that worked with him on the show, the bigger it made *The Jack Benny Show*, and the bigger man it made of Jack Benny.

So, all these ingredients went into building a solid, top rate, completely accepted performance on the part of everyone. And that was one of the reasons why Jack was on top for the many, many years that he was. Does that answer your question?

Mel   Just so beautifully it answers my question.

D.W.   Well, I've carried on a long while, sort of around the bush to get to the point. But it's all there to be said.

Mel   I want to ask you one last question. I also recall you being the announcer for *The Baby Snooks Show*.

D.W.   That's right. [Laughs]

Mel   I remember you were sponsored by Tums!

D.W.   T-U-M-S, Tums for the Tummy!

Mel   Tell us about your association personally with Fanny Brice.

D.W.   I had no personal association with Fanny at all. As a matter of fact, I only met her briefly before I went to do that show. But let me tell you a little story that might be amusing. It was embarrassing to me at the time.

Let me set the picture. You have to remember now that Fanny has been off the air for two years. She and Frank Morgan did the old show for Maxwell House Coffee. They each did a half hour for Maxwell House. Now Fanny was off the air for two years, and she's coming back on as a sole performer. *The Baby Snooks Show*. On the opening show, I had a very declamatory billboard, cold billboard: "*The Baby Snooks Show*, starring Fanny Brice." So what comes out on the opening show, I hope I can foul it up and remember, "The Baby Shooks Show, starring Fanny Brice."

Well, the control room, all the engineers, the directors, the producers, and everybody else fell apart. I fell apart. I had to laugh at my own stupidity. Then we started all over again and got off on the right track. But for the entire rest of the season, it was like a water hole on a golf course. I had to be sure I didn't repeat it.

Mel   That's great. Don, I want to thank you very much. You're a gentleman, and I appreciate your time. This was a delightful interview.

D.W.   You're welcome. And thank you very much.

Frank Nelson

The Jack Benny Show

Mel   Frank, very few people ever made me laugh like the wonderful character that you portrayed on *The Jack Benny Show*. I want to start at the beginning and ask you what you did prior to working with Benny on radio, and how you got started on *The Jack Benny Show*, and how you got started with that character.

F.N.   Well, that's kind of a long complicated question, the way you put it. Actually, before I worked with Jack, I was a dramatic actor. I started out at KOA in Denver, Colorado, in 1925.

Then I did a series in Denver. I was in high school at the time. I went for an audition and they said, "Oh no, you're much too young."

And I said, "Oh well, thank you," and started to leave. And they said, "Have you ever read on a microphone?" I said, "No, I haven't."

They said, "Would you like to, as long as you made the trip here?"

I said, "Yes, that sounds like a nice idea." So I went in. There were 30 of us to audition. The next day they called back 12. The following day they called back four. And the following day they called me and told me I had it.

So I worked that show for about 26 weeks. Then I worked for KFEL, which was another local station in Denver. I announced, I sold time, I did a little bit of this and that.

Frank Nelson

Then I decided to go out to the coast and try for pictures. So I came out to the West Coast. In the early days I didn't do very well in pictures. I did a little extra work. Then I started working for KNX, which was across from Paramount and RKO.

Georgia Fifield, I guess, gave me my first job out there. She was an actress and also she cast shows, local shows that we got $5 for. So I worked for Georgia.

Then I went to work down at KFI. I did a lot of dramatic things. I did *Dark Canyon*, *The Three Musketeers*, I did *Makers of History*, which was about early American history.

Then slowly, very slowly, things began to happen out there on a national level. First there was a show over on the RKO lot that was called *The RKO Theater of the Air*. That was not a sponsored show. It was kind of an in-house show for RKO. I announced that show. I played parts. I did whatever was necessary.

They'd have stars coming in, for instance, to do a scene. Well, if they didn't show up, I'd play that too. Whatever there was, I did. Then we did the first show out of there that was sponsored. It was a thing called *Fly Wheel Shyster and Fly Wheel*. It featured Groucho Marx and Chico Marx. It was done on a motion picture soundstage.

Then one day I got a call. This was in June of 1934. They called me and said, "We want you to do an insert spot with Jack Benny." So I went down and did this five-minute spot. It was kind of a cute little spot. We were on a train, coming out to the coast, and Jack is putting on the dog about the fact that he's going to Hollywood, and he's going to make his fortune in Hollywood, and his importance and so on.

And Jack says to me, "You know, I'm gonna be in pictures. You seem like a personable young man. Possibly I can do something for you. My name is Jack Benny. What's yours?"

And I said, "Clark Gable," and that was the joke! So to make a long story short, that's how I started with Jack. Then when Jack brought his regular show out, I just did various parts with him.

You asked how the character started. Well, one day they merely wrote in a "yes," and I happened to stress that yes a little, and it got a laugh. So the next week they had me on again, and the writer said, "Hey, let's do that thing again." I said, "What thing?" He said, "Well, you know, last week you said 'yes,' and it got a laugh because you stretched it out." And I said, "Oh, yeah."

So I thought, what the devil did I do? And I wasn't quite sure. So then I stretched it a little more, and out of it grew the character. It was a long and lovely relationship.

Mel   How many years did you work with Jack?

F.N.   Thirty-seven years.

Mel   I guess most people associate you with the character the floor
         walker.

F.N.   Yes, I think the first set thing that we did was when Jack walked
         up to me and he said, "Mister, oh mister?" And I said, "Yeeessss?"
         And he said, "Are you the floor walker?" And I said, "Who do
         you think I am with this carnation in my button hole, a flower-
         pot?" And that was the original floor walker joke.

Mel   You also did the same character as a train station clerk.

F.N.   Yes, anytime he met me, it was a funny thing; I never had a name
         on the show. For instance, if for any reason a name was necessary,
         he's say, "Well, I'll call him Mr. Nelson, because that's his name."

         Mel Blanc was Professor LeBlanc. That was a character written as
         Professor LeBlanc, the violin teacher. Well, I never had that kind
         of identification. So it was just always the fella that was his nem-
         esis. He used to call me his nemesis on the show.

Mel   So many, many laughs. As you think back, do you have any memo-
         rable thoughts or perhaps an anecdote or two that you could
         relate?

F.N.   Well, there are a number of things that stick in my memory.
         One, Jack is a real human being as a person. The only broadcast I
         ever missed in my life was when we went to New York City,
         during the war years. It was in the dead of winter. I woke up the
         day of the show, and I was sick as a dog. I staggered out of bed.
         The doctor came up and said, "You have a fever of 104. You're
         not going anywhere. You're staying here."

I said, "Yes, sir." And so, later in the afternoon came rehearsal time, and I got out of bed and went to rehearsal. I did the first broadcast, and I guess I was so stuffed up that when I did the loud thing of "Yeeesssss," to me, I couldn't hear it. I thought my voice broke, and it didn't come out.

At the end of the show, I walked up and said, "Oh God, Jack, I'm so sorry. I'm sorry that I loused up the show." And he said, "What do you mean?" I said, "Well, my voice, it broke." He said, "Your voice didn't break. What are you talking about?"

And then it dawned on him that there was something wrong. So he found out I was sick. So I got back to the hotel and got back to bed, waiting for the repeat show. At that time, we did the second show live; it wasn't done on tape. We didn't even have tape then. We had transcriptions, just coming in, but we weren't using them.

Jack walked into my room and said, "You know, you had no business coming to the rehearsal, none at all. No business doing the show. And you're not to do the show tonight. One of the writers will play your part." And that's the only broadcast that I ever missed in my whole career, in all the years that I've been in the business. And as I said, I started in 1926.

So I protested loudly and got nowhere, of course. And Jack said, "I forbid you to come to the show, and you're not to come." Now after the show was over he came up and said, "Look, Frank, would you mind if I called your wife and tell her that you're okay and that we're taking care of you and so on?"

And I said, "Oh, I think that would be lovely, Jack." And so he went down, he called my wife. He talked to her for over an hour. Then he came back up. He said, "Now, you're to stay in bed until you're ready to go home."

He had nurses around the clock for me for a week. Before he left, he tossed a check on the bed, and it was for double what he had told me I was to be paid for going to New York. He said, "That's for getting sick," and he walked out of the room.

Now, when I got out of that bed, with nurses around the clock and all, I went down to the lobby. I thought, boy, this is gonna be a bill. I got down there, and they said, "Oh, there are no bills. Everything has been taken care of."

Mr. Benny had taken care of the whole thing. So that's the kind of a human being he was. He was a warm and wonderful man. He did many wonderful things. His charity things, where he gave to charity, one of the stipulations he'd have when he gave large amounts was don't give me any publicity. I don't want publicity. He was that kind of a human being.

Mel   That says a lot for Jack Benny.

F.N.   Yeah, you know I don't think I have ever seen, in my whole life, such an outpouring of love for a man as I saw after his death. People called all of us who were on the show from around the country. They called from little radio stations. They called from places that you would say, well, if they did a quarter hour in tribute to Jack Benny that would be quite an accomplishment. They were doing three- and four- and five-hour shows as a tribute to Jack Benny.

Mel   I was on one of them. *The Larry Glick Show* on WBZ radio. It was a very memorable evening.

F.N.   Well, it was really marvelous that people felt that strongly. I think there was a feeling all over the country that they had lost something special.

Mel   I have not seen such a reaction with the death of any other entertainer, including Al Jolson, including Judy Garland.

F.N.   That's right.

Mel   Nobody quite reacted the way they did with Jack's passing.

F.N.   That's right. I worked with both of them. I worked with Judy and I worked with Al. I worked with Al quite a bit in the early days.

Mel   Was it *The Shell Chateau*?

F.N.   Yes, *The Shell Chateau* was a show that I announced. It was a fun show to do, and I did it for two years.

Mel   How about *Baby Snooks*? What role did you play?

F.N.   On *Baby Snooks* I did not play a regular role. I worked the show regularly. I was on week after week. Phil Rapp was the writer, and somehow Phil liked me, I guess. So there was a part for me. I don't think I missed two broadcasts that I can remember. My very dear friend, and the former husband of my wife, who passed away in 1968, was Hanley Stafford. He played Baby Snooks' father.

         Of course, Hanley and I worked together on the *Blondie* show also. He was, of course, Mr. Dithers, and I played Herb Woodley, the next door neighbor. So we had a long, close association. He was a very fine gentleman. He was another fine actor, I might add.

Mel   I guess your fondest memories really are with *The Benny Show*.

F.N.   Well, I guess it is my longest memory of all. You know, when you have a job for 37 years, you're not sure if it will last, but you stick in there. It was a long and beautiful association. There are many things that I remember in the radio days that I found charming.

         One thing, for an actor, I don't think there was a better period in the whole world, for an actor than radio. You could do anything that your voice would allow you to do. You could be an old man, a young man, a Frenchman, a Scotchman, whatever you could play. You could do all the dialects, all the characters. It didn't matter if you were fat or thin, tall or slim, or whether you were baldheaded or had big, bushy hair. Nothing mattered. It was all in the voice. So it was a daily challenge.

Unlike television, where they'll make 22 shows and repeat them three times in a year, where you see it over and over again til you're sick of it, radio was a business that came alive in the morning and it died at night. It was new day after day after day. We didn't do repeats. It was a rare instance where they ever took anything off the shelf and redid it.

Now, of course, you're pulling all those things off the shelf, and we hear them everywhere. In those days it was a new and fresh approach every day. So it was a wonderful, wonderful challenge for a performer.

Mel   You know, Frank, we get to see you on television a lot in Boston, because they're running the old Benny shows.

F.N.   Oh, really? Are they doing those now?

Mel   Yes, and you absolutely kill me. You kill me.

F.N.   [Laughs] Of course, you know, the association that we had was much stronger in the radio days. To me, the highlight of *The Benny Show* was the radio shows. I think that there was a skilled craftsmanship on everybody's part, in that day, that did not necessarily exist in the television days.

Mel   I agree with you.

F.N.   In the first place, you had a cast that was a regular cast. You knew all these people. They weren't in every show, but they were in a great majority of the shows. The audience was in on it. The second Jack said, "Mister, oh mister…," they knew I was coming on.

If a fella said, "Hey, bud," they said, "Oh, here's the race track tout." So the audience had an association with these characters.

The audience was in on the joke.

When Jack went to television, quite properly, he wanted to spread out and to do different things. So the regular characters that you had known throughout the radio days, they only came in every sixth or seventh show. The rest of the shows were all different. So it wasn't quite the same on TV as it was on radio.

Mel   Well, I wanted to thank you very much, Frank. It's been a delight. I think I went over the 10-minute mark. I promised you 10 minutes!

F.N.   You know, I knew when you said it that with my mouth it would never end up in 10 minutes. So I wouldn't criticize you in the world for that.

Mel   All I can say to you, Frank, in all seriousness, is that you are terrific, both professionally and personally. I got to spend a lot of time with you last night, and you are something else. Your wife is a doll.

F.N.   Thank you. I think she's kind of cute myself!

Mel   I want to end by asking you one question.

F.N.   Yes.

Mel   This is my favorite question: Mister, oh mister ...

F.N.   Yeeesssss? [Laughs]

Mel   Thank you very much, Frank.

F.N.   Thank you.

Mel Blanc

The Jack Benny Show,
The Mel Blanc Show, The Cisco Kid

Mel   Mel, I'd like to talk basically about radio, and how you started and how it all came about with you on radio.

M.B.   Okay, I'll be glad to tell you. I started in 1927. I was just getting out of high school. I sang a song on radio station KGW, and this was for a program called the *Hoot Owls*, which was a charitable show that helped people who needed food and clothing immediately.

Mel   Where was that station located?

M.B.   Portland, Oregon. They would call in and tell us that they knew a family that needs food or clothing. We, in turn, would call the Sunshine Division of the Portland Police, who sent out a car immediately with food and clothing for the people. That was the first job I ever had on the radio.

Eventually, they made me a member of the degree team. They made me the Grand Snicker. This went on for a good many years. In the meantime, I had been in music, and I played with the staff band there at KGW. I eventually became the musical director of the Orpheum Theatre there, which played vaudeville acts.

I was then called down to San Francisco to be a master of ceremonies of a program called *Road Show*. It was a national show, NBC. I did that til it was over, for about a year.

Mel Blanc

Then I went down to Los Angeles, where I had a very miserable time trying to find work. Although I had been successful in the Northwest, it was very tough to get a job in Los Angeles. I did several small shows, but then I had an offer to come back to Portland and do a show called *Cobwebs and Nuts*.

Now this show I had to write—it was six one-hour shows a week—and do all the voices on the show. Not having gotten a job in Los Angeles, I did the next best thing—I got married!

Mel   What year was that?

M.B.   It was 1933. Well, she came back with me to Portland, and I worked on this program for two years. They told me they would pay me more for each sponsor I had. After the first three weeks, I had 11 sponsors. They started me out at $15. I said, "Look, you guys said you were gonna give me more money." They said, "Okay, we'll give you more money." The next week they gave me a raise— I got $20!

I then worked for the Portland Breakfast Club, which gave me an additional $10—kept us alive, anyway. This went on for two years. They were too cheap to hire any orchestras or any side men to fill in the little parts. I had to do all the parts myself, all the voices. This is where I learned most of my voices. Quite amazing that I could learn so much in these two years.

They wouldn't allow me to hire a female for the show, so I had to use my wife. So finally, after working 16 hours a day, after two years of this crazy show, my wife said, "What do you want, a nervous breakdown, or do you want to go back to Los Angeles?" I said, "We better go back."

So we went back to Los Angeles. The first job I got paid me more than I made all week in Portland.

Mel   What was the station?

M.B.   It was KFWB for Johnny Murray. From there I went to a program called the *Joe Penner Show*. Remember Joe Penner? I worked on quite a few of his shows. Then, eventually I worked with Al Pearce. I worked on his show for quite a while, and during that time I worked other radio shows.

One of the shows I worked was *The Jack Benny Show*. Jack called me in. He had a bear in the basement who was guarding the vault. The bear had eaten the gas man or something.

Mel   What year was this?

M.B.   This was in 1940. Well, previous to that time, I tried for a year
        and a half to get an audition with what was then Schlesinger
        Cartoons. The guy kept saying to me, "I'm sorry, we have all the
        voices we need."

        So I kept going back every two weeks and saying, "At least listen
        to me," and he wouldn't do it. Finally, after a year and a half, this
        guy died! So I went to the next man in charge, his name was
        Tregg Brown. I auditioned for him, and he said, "Great. Would
        you do it again for the directors?"

        I said, "Sure." So I auditioned for them. They liked it. One of
        them said, "Can you do a drunken bull who is in one of my
        pictures?"

        So I had to think fast. I said, "Yeah, I think I can." He said, "How
        would he sound?"

        I said, [Mel Blanc imitates drunken bull]. He said, "Great, you're
        on next week!" So that was the first job I did in cartoons. And
        then I started doing Porky Pig and Bugs Bunny, Daffy Duck,
        Tweety, Sylvester, and a few hundred others.

        So, Jack Benny heard me at the shows, and he called me in and
        asked me if I could do this bear, this Carmichael, who he had
        down in the basement guarding his vault.

        So I said, "Yeah, I think I can." He said, "Well, what would he
        sound like?"

        I said, "A little like this. [M.B. imitates a bear.] He said, "Great,
        you're on next week."

        So for six months, that's all I did, was the growl of a bear. Finally,
        I said to him, "You know, Mr. Benny, I can also talk!"

        Well, you know Jack. He pounded the table. He said, "Great, I'll
        have the writers write something in for you." So one of the first
        things I did was the train calling. You know: "Train leaving on
        Track 5 for Anaheim, Azusa, and Cucamonga."

Mel Blanc and Jackson Beck

Then Jack brought in a parrot, and he said, "Make him talk!"

So I said, "Okay." I said, [M.B. imitates parrot]. He said, "Good, we'll use it."

And then the writers would always try to throw me a curve. They'd write something in the script that they thought I couldn't do. Like we were visiting Epson Downs in England, you know, the race track. Milt Josefsberg, one of the writers for Benny, he writes in: "Mel Blanc does an English horse whiney." That's not easy to do. How are you gonna tell what nationality a horse is? So I said okay.

So I came to that spot, and not wanting to say no to anything, I did an English horse whiney. It sounded a little like this. [M.B. imitates English horse.]

Jack, again, pounded the table. He said, "Keep it in!"

And of course, he brought in many other characters. His Maxwell stopping and dying and so on. I kept working with Jack til the very end. I was on almost all of his shows.

One of the most important things that Jack ever had on his show was the Si-Sy routine.

Mel   Mel, it is priceless!

M.B.   And there is only about 10 words of dialogue in the whole thing. [M.B. does Si-Sy routine.]

This routine would break Jack up every time. At all rehearsals, Jack would break up. We'd have to stop, you know, and re-time it again. And he'd say, "Okay, I'm not going to laugh anymore. I won't laugh on the show." But, by God, every show that we did he broke up on, on this one little routine.

We started that on radio, and we kept it going on television for a good many years.

I finally opened my own company. It's called Blanc Communications Corporation. We do commercials. I made my son, Noel, the president of the company. He has produced over 4,000 commercials.

Mel   Mel, as you think back, what are your special memories about Jack Benny? Any special thoughts?

M.B.   Yes, he was a wonderful man. And a very kind and considerate person. Not too many people knew him like I did. I had a very bad automobile accident about 14 years ago. Jack came to see me at the hospital almost every day. I was unconscious for 21 days. But Jack was there, hoping I'd come out of it, you know.

When I did come out of it, why the first person I saw was Jack. I said, "Jack, what the heck are you doing here?"

He said, "I just came by to see how you were!"

Well, I was in the hospital for two months and Jack came back a couple times a week to see me. Then I was brought home in a full-body cast. Jack would come out to see me. One week he comes out and knocks on the front door. My wife opens the door and Jack says, "Is Mel home?"

He was just a wonderful guy. I've worked with practically every star in the business, but I've never run across a man who was as wonderful as Jack.

Mel   That's a lovely thing to say.

M.B.   Yes, it really is true. I just loved the guy, really.

Mel   It kind of came through. It was obvious.

M.B.   Yeah, well you know, I think Jack loved me too, because through all his sincerity, he always wondered how I was doing, how I was getting along. He had so much interest in me. I don't think he had it with too many people. It was just a very strong friendship that we had.

Mel   It was an association, I'm gonna guess, for 23 or 24 years?

M.B.   Since 1938.

Mel   Well, I want to thank you very much.

M.B.   Thank you. It's been a pleasure talking to you.

Jackson Beck
Superman, The Cisco Kid

Mel   I'm sitting here with a gentleman that I have admired for many years as the Cisco Kid and the announcer on *Superman*, and that is Jackson Beck. Jackson, your voice is well known. Anybody that hears your voice, that knows radio, immediately knows it's you.

J.B.   Well, that's very flattering. Thank you.

Mel   And I'd like to ask you how it all began, your radio career?

J.B.   Well, you won't believe it. I answered an ad in the paper.

Mel   You're kidding.

J.B.   Well, I had done a lot of amateur theater and community center stuff ever since I was a kid. And we started doing things for the Red Cross and charity things. I was a little bit of a kid. I always had the bug. My father was an actor for a while in silent movies and so on. So, you know, it was the depth of the Depression, and we were all out of work anyway. I saw an ad in the paper saying: "You too can become a radio actor or an announcer."

So I answered the ad, and it was down in the Bond Building, which is where all the agents had offices. I don't know, there might have been a few good ones in there, but 99% of them were con men. But,

Jackson Beck as TheCisco Kid

anyhow, I answered this ad, and I go into this place, and it's draped in purple velvet. They give me a script, and I read this silly thing. They come out and say, "You're really great, but you need a little polish. You should take some lessons. We're gonna recommend a school. It will cost you $50." At that point, I didn't even have 50 cents, much less $50. So I said, "Look, if you think I'm that talented, you know, why don't you manage me and instead of the 10%, I'll give you 20%." Well, they couldn't exactly see it that way. And so, you know, I was pretty smart. I knew it was a con. At any rate, in spite of that, I went around to this school to see what was going on there. I didn't have $50 – believe me, I didn't have it. I got talking to the guy that ran the school, and it worked out this way: I became an instructor, right away. No salary. Maybe a commission on the people who came in. Then I started, you know, having been around a little bit, I had a vague idea where to go to look for work. So, I started meeting people, and hanging around agents' offices, and eventually one little thing leads to another. Another out-of-work actor tells you where they are hiring or doing something.

So I went after Broadway, and went after the movies, and finally I got a thing on radio. I started out working for nothing at WNYC and WFAB and WVF, and a whole bunch of stations which are no longer in existence. And I learned my craft that way. I guess it was an investment in the future, working for nothing like that.

At any rate, eventually I broke through, and I got a job for money. I guess I did a pretty good job, and I got recommended from them on to other things. The first job I had was doing an impersonation of John Payne for a promo record for Columbia Pictures. And I used to do a lot of impersonations. You do many strange things when you're a hungry actor. Oh, I don't know, somebody heard that, and liked it, and recommended me for another job, and I did quite a few of those things. Then you start trading information with other people in the same position you are. Eventually it leads to things.

The first network show I ever did was *Death Valley Days*, which was an experience, because, it may sound funny, you know, we did it in formal dress. It was in front of an audience, also dressed in black tie. The whole thing, looking back, was so pretentious, it was ridiculous. But here you were, a disembodied voice going over the air, and you had to wear black tie!

Well, that's how the thing started, and you just kind of mushroomed from there, as careers do. What else?

Mel   Well, I associate you, as I mentioned, primarily with being the announcer on *Superman* and *The Cisco Kid*. Could you tell us about those two shows?

J.B.   Well, yeah. I had done a good many shows, and I knew a good many people by the time I got connected with *Superman*, which was somewhere around 1938. I did it for about 15 years, until we went off in 1953. That is the radio show.

Years later we did the cartoon film, which is, I'm sure, playing around somewhere. And we've done albums and all that. I was known pretty much by that time as a narrator, announcer, actor, and fairly versatile. I had been on the show playing parts, and I don't know, one way or the other I was auditioned for the job, and I got it. I stayed with it until the very end. That is, *Superman*.

That was a marvelous show. Bud Collyer, of course, was Superman, and I, in addition to doing the narration, doubled in a lot of parts. I played many collections of heavies and Nazis; you know the war came along about then. I played Japanese villains — you know that was standard fare in those days. I also played Beanie, the office boy in a high Henry Aldrich-type voice, along with Jackie Kelk, who played Jimmy Olsen. And you know, I was his buddy, and kind of like the second kid on the show.

So, it was a great experience, and *Cisco*, well it seems like I spent half my life at WOR, I guess about 20 years of it. I was there every day. It was a marvelous relationship, and it lasted until, unfortunately, radio folded up. I have done a great deal of character work, and I did *The Cisco Kid* for the Ziv Organization, which owns the script. I had done a number of other things for them in the past. So they knew that I could do the dialect. I guess they had confidence in me as an actor. They gave me the part, and I played that for three or four years until it moved to California, when somebody else took over the part.

And that was a great and enjoyable show. When I did the show, it was very heavily romantic. There was always a girl on the show, to whom I said, "Of all the senoritas I have ever known, you are the most beautiful. On my heart, I swear it!"

And there would be a harp run from the orchestra, and she'd say, "Oh, Cisco!"

And you knew I was making love to her. I had a different leading lady every week. It was a great deal of fun. Marvelous show. We had the old Longines Symphonette as my background music. So how could you miss? And we had a marvelous bunch of people on the show, and a good director, Jack MacGregor. We had good writers. We had John Sinn, who originated the show, then Kenny Lyons, and then a group of other people who came afterward and wrote the show. It was all very beautiful until it went to California, and there they changed it into a kind of cowboy-detective sort of thing. They lost the essence of the original show, I thought. But of course that's only my opinion. But I enjoyed it tremendously. The fan mail was great. I used to get all of these crazy letters from lonely women. You know, it was pretty good. I guess it came off rather well. Anyhow, I enjoyed it.

Mel   Do you have any particular fond memories or anecdotes you could perhaps relate in regard to either *Cisco* or the *Superman* show?

J.B.   Well, there were so many things about *Superman*. We used to break each other up, and we'd wind up on the floor. The only things that were kind of double entendre and little boo boos in the script, which were read for laughs and carried over the air sometimes. Of course, an actor's greatest fear, in radio, was dead air. So some strange things happened when people dropped scripts or somebody forgets to get up on mike, or somebody makes a boo boo and mispronounces a word. And that sets the whole thing off. We had a marvelous character actor on there, Julian Noa, who played Perry White, the editor. His favorite expression was poppycock. That was written in the script. He would always say, "Oh, poppycock!"

One day, for some reason or other, he separated the two words "poppy cock," and had suddenly thought he'd said a dirty word. He tried to cover it, and by the time he got through, it was pandemonium. We were all on the floor. He was up there flustered. He kept on repeating the word. I don't know how much time we lost. But finally the director signaled the organist to come in, and that ended that. And then after the commercial we came back.

But it was pandemonium, and I don't think we could face each other for the next three days. Absolutely incredible!

Mel   I also enjoy you, many times, on the *CBS Radio Mystery Theater*. Do you enjoy working that?

J.B.   Yes, I've done a few of them. I enjoy working it, because I enjoy doing radio. Anybody who ever was in radio enjoys the opportunity of coming back and doing the same things again. You know it brings back a lot of memories. But, you know, you can't live in the past. What you worry about right now is: what am I doing today, what am I doing tomorrow? The nostalgia bit is all very well, but today is reality.

Yeah, I enjoy the *Mystery Theater*. I think some of the shows are really excellent, well done.

Mel   Do you fly out to the coast for that, or do you do that in New York?

J.B.   No, that's done in New York at CBS. Hy Brown directs it and produces it.

Mel   Well, Jackson Beck, I want to thank you very much. It's been a delight to talk to you. I appreciate your time immensely.

J.B.   Well, thank you very much for having me here. I've enjoyed it.

Harold Peary
The Great Gildersleeve

H.P.   Hello!

Mel   Oh, I know that voice!

H.P.   You do? Who's this?

Mel   This is Mel Simons calling from Boston, Mass., Mr. Peary.

H.P.   Oh, yes.

Mel   And I would know your voice anywhere.

H.P.   Well, thank you.

Mel   I'm a longtime fan of both you and the Great Gildersleeve.

H.P.   [Laughs] Well, thank you.

Mel   I'm a regular on the TV show on Boston, talking about old-time radio, and I often talk about you.

Harold Peary

H.P.   Well, good. I'm glad to hear that.

Mel   And the public responds tremendously when I mention Hal Peary and the Great Gildersleeve.

H.P.   That's fine. That's what I like to hear.

Mel   I'd love to ask you a few questions, if I may.

H.P.   Sure, I'd be delighted to answer anything you have.

Mel   Well, my great memories of you, growing up, were Wednesday nights at 8:30, sponsored by Kraft.

H.P.   That's right.

Mel   I never missed you.

H.P.   Oh, good.

Mel   I loved your laugh.

H.P.   [Laughs the Gildy laugh.] That's the one!

Mel   Oh, that's great. Your show was a spin-off. I think you were the first of the spin-offs, weren't you?

H.P.   Yes, I was. I was the first actual spin-off from a big-time show.

Mel   Could you talk a little bit about it?

H.P.   I joined *Fibber McGee and Molly* in 1937 in Chicago. In 1938, Molly became quite ill. She was off the show for about six months. It was practically Fibber McGee and Company at that point.

So they took all the characters, or stooges as we used to call them in those days, and kind of built them up. Throckmorton P. Gildersleeve, who was then called George Gildersleeve, was made a next door neighbor.

The name George Gildersleeve didn't seem to kind of click, you know. It wasn't the right thing. So Don Quinn, who's the genius who wrote that show and created it, said, "What's the name of that street you live on?"

And I said, "Throckmorton Place." He said, "Throckmorton P. Gildersleeve. That's your new name!"

Don was crazy about names, to begin with. The first thing I ever did for him on the show was a Chinese laundry man called Goory Fooey. He loved names.

"Anyway," he said, "we'll try that." So the next week I was Throckmorton P. Gildersleeve instead of George Gildersleeve. We were having some difficulty, at the end of the show, Jim and I. We, Jim Jordan and I, were adlibbing.

One night, the producer of the show, Bruce Kamman, gave us the old signal to stretch. So we started to adlib a little bit. I had already used an expression called Little Chum, you know. But I hadn't added the laugh which I intended to do someday, if the opportunity presented itself. So I said, "Well, Little Chum," cause we had been having a little fight.

I said, "Well, Little Chum," and then I threw in a laugh which I had started in San Francisco many years ago. [Gildy laughs.] We were in a theater called Studio A. We all had audiences in those days. Our audience consisted of 600 people. Well, the audience screamed. So Mr. Kamman held up his hand and put up two fingers. That meant do it again. So I did it again, and we almost didn't get off the air. The audience loved it.

So the next week, of course, I was kind of the number-one stooge. And Throckmorton P. Gildersleeve, and the laugh, became a steady thing. Well, that was back in Chicago. Then we all went to California in 1939. I was instrumental in getting them to California, because I'm a Californian, you know.

Cecil Underwood was brought to California to be our producer. So we came to California in '39, and then in '41 it became the number-one show on radio. Bob Hope and Red Skelton were trailing behind us. You can quote me, by the way. [Laughs.]

Mel   Thank you, I will.

H.P.   So in 1941, Marian and Jim Jordan wanted to take a longer vacation then they usually had. They usually took off six weeks. They wanted to take off 13. So the agency came to me and said, "Hal, you're so hot right now, maybe you can think of something for a summer replacement."

I said, "You're kidding." I only had about four weeks to do this. Well, a man by the name of Leonard Levinson, who was then the assistant to Don Quinn, and I got together. We sat around for about a week, trying to figure out what we were going to do.

And finally Leonard Levinson, who knew a great deal about me, said, "Aren't you raising a couple of kids?"

I said, "Yes, I have a niece and a nephew that I'm raising. They're my wife's sister's children, and they're orphans. What do you mean?"

He said, "What a great idea!"

So I said, "But they're just little kids."

He said, "Well, let's work on that. So we did. We put together a show where Throckmorton P. Gildersleeve, who had owned the Gild Girdle Works in Wistful Vista, would go to another town. The new town was called Summerfield. He would take over the adoption of a couple of children. They would be his niece and nephew.

Now the children were entirely different from what I was raising. I had a couple of little kids. The boy would be about 12, and the girl would be about 17. This was kind of an interesting thing to work with. So anyway, we put a show together. Gildersleeve left Wistful Vista, and the Girdle Works employees would come and give him a briefcase. And the briefcase, of course, was what caused all the trouble.

When he got on the train, he got into a fight with an old guy who he thought stole his briefcase. It turned out to be Judge

Hooker, who was the man that he was to appear before in Summerfield the next day to take over the custody of these two children. There's the plot.

So Judge Hooker said, when he saw him, "Well, I'm gonna take at least 10 weeks to make you prove to me that you're worthy of these children." Now this was supposed to be the 13 weeks that we were to be on the air, you see.

Well, what happened was, Mr. Johnson, of Johnson's Wax, who sponsored *Fibber McGee and Molly*, he thought our show was just great when we auditioned it. Everybody else did too. But he wanted Ransom Sherman. Now you may be too young to remember Ransom Sherman.

Mel   No, I do remember Ransom Sherman.

H.P.   Good, well he wanted Ransom Sherman that he used to listen to every afternoon. Mr. Johnson was an unusual sort of a man, to begin with. I may go on record by saying that I didn't think he should have been the head of Johnson's Wax.

Well, anyway, he wanted Ransom Sherman. So even though the show was a big success, I was sort of happy, because I was ready to go on to do the summer replacement for *Fibber McGee and Molly*. We already had one script.

So when they said, "We're gonna put on Ransom Sherman," I said, "Great."

So our family took off for Glacier National Park on a vacation. And while I was in Glacier National Park, a ranger came to me and said, "Are you Mr. Gildersleeve?"

And I said, "Not really." But I said, "But I play a part."

He said, "We've been looking for somebody by the name of Gildersleeve. What is your real name?"

I said, "Peary."

He said, "Oh, wonderful."

He said, "I want you to come down and place a call to Chicago, because they've been after you for three days."

Well, I went and placed the call. We were in Glacier National Park, you know. Went down and placed the call to Chicago, and they said, "Well, you didn't go on for *Fibber McGee and Molly*, but we've sold you to Kraft as a nighttime show for a year."

Well, you know, this is something unusual. Here I was going to replace somebody for the summer, and they dumped me, and now somebody wants me for the fall on a show of my own.

And I said, "Well, what do I do now?"

They said, "You'd better come back and start writing."

Well, I did, you know. I went back, and Mr. Levinson and I wrote the first year together. We also had a couple of other assistants. We finally got enough shows to go ahead with our show, and we went on the air.

We were on Sundays, just before *Jack Benny*. But we followed *The Catholic Hour*. *The Catholic Hour* had a two-point rating, and *Benny* had something like a 10 or 11. We had to come in there someplace between them. Well, anyway, we survived, and after that we were put on Wednesdays.

I was on for 11 years, and then when I left the show, a fellow by the name of Willard Waterman did a fair job of impersonating me. He did the show for another five or six years, I think, on radio without a sponsor. NBC owned the show, and they kept it on just because they were nasty. [Gildy laughs.]

Mel   That laugh kills me.

H.P.   Good. Anyway, I'm just kidding about that. Anyway, Willard did the television show, and unfortunately it wasn't very good. I was upset about that too. I wanted to do the television show. One of the reasons I quit doing the radio show was because I wanted to buy the Gildersleeve name, which I didn't really own, because it started on *Fibber McGee and Molly*. So many other people owned it.

But anyway, that's what happened. I was the first spin-off. I'm very happy about that.

Mel   You know, I talk about that on television. With all the spin-offs on television....

H.P.   I hope you're recording this? I guess you are.

Mel   Yes, yes I am, and I tell people that the first of the spin-offs was you. And then I think Beulah was also a spin-off, wasn't she. Wasn't she the maid?

H.P.   Beulah was long after me.

Mel   What are your fondest memories of the show, as you think back?

H.P.   Well, I think that the fondest memory that I have is because I hired a lot of people that were radio actors that I knew. People like Walter Tetley. Walter Tetley was, you know, on *Fred Allen*, and he was on a great many things in New York.

Mel   Phil Harris, Alice Faye, he was on also I recall.

H.P.   That's right. He came to Hollywood, and he was on a lot of shows here. I was instrumental on getting him on *Fibber McGee*, because I knew him. Then when I wanted somebody to play Leroy, who was supposed to be about a 12-year-old boy, I realized here's a kid about 17 or 18 then, but he still had that voice.

          Not only Walter Tetley, Leroy, but there was an old friend of mine from Chicago that I knew by the name of Earle Ross. He played Judge Hooker.

Mel   Oh, yes, of course.

H.P.   Now, Earle Ross was a man who had a very nice voice, and he was rather dramatic. As a matter of fact, he owned his own legit company under canvas. I don't think you know what under canvas is in the legitimate theater.

Mel   No.

H.P.   It's a tent show. All these people worked in show business in tents.

There was a man, years ago, that worked with me in a tent. He was the star, and I was just a kid actor. His name was Richard LeGrand. I had known him for years. I worked with him in that little company, and then I worked with him in radio in San Francisco. He became Mr. Peavey.

Now, Mr. Peavey, after I put him into that role, I taught him to say, "Well now, I wouldn't say that." These are my greatest moments.

Then there was a little gal by the name of Shirley Mitchell. She used to live with Dinah Shore. I wanted Dinah Shore to play Leila Ransom.

Mel   Your girlfriend.

H.P.   Yes, but Dinah said, "No, I sing. I don't know if I want to be an actress." Shirley Mitchell was one of her roommates, in those days there were three or four of them. One of them was Kitty Kallen. You remember her!

Mel   Sure, the singer.

H.P.   Well, the girls were rooming together. They were all friends. Shirley Mitchell said to me, "Well, I think I can do Dinah."

Shirley was an actress. She said, "I think I can do Dinah better than she can." I said, "Why don't you come down and prove it?"

So she came down one day, and that's where Leila came from. She played a Southern widow.

All the characters were something that we developed. These were the greatest moments that I had on the Gildersleeve show.

Mel   How did you start on *Fibber McGee and Molly*? How did that character come to be originally?

H.P.   I'll tell you what happened. I was on so many shows in those days in Chicago. I was doing 17 or 18 shows in Chicago when I went to work for *Fibber McGee*. The only reason I was able to work for *Fibber McGee* was they switched from Monday to Tuesday. Originally they were on Monday opposite *The Lux Radio Theater*. And they were being killed in the ratings. *The Lux Radio Theater* was one of the biggest shows in the business. But then they switched to Tuesday. I was able to do it because on Monday I was doing three shows. So I was able to do a few parts. Those were the days when Perry Como and the Ted Weems Orchestra were on the show. I was able to go on the show occasionally and do a bit and then run to do some of the other shows. Then finally when it came on Tuesdays, I was able to go on and do a few characters. I had been on *Girl Alone* with Betty Winkler. I was doing seven characters on a show called *Tom Mix*.

Mel   Of course. Is Curley Bradley still living?

H.P.   He's out here. I don't know if he's still living. He's much younger than I am.

Mel   I haven't heard of Curley Bradley in years.

H.P.   I know he's out of show business. Do you know that when I was on *Tom Mix*, after the famous trio left us, which was the Ranch Boys, Curley Bradley was then a member of the Ranch Boys?

Mel   No, I didn't know that.

H.P.   They left us, and the man who was doing Tom Mix and I, and a kid who was about 16 years old, I think, we had to do the theme song. The kid that was 16 years old was George Gobel.

Mel   Wow!

H.P.   Oh yeah.

Mel   I never knew that. What a great hunk of nostalgia that is.

H.P.   I'll tell you who was doing Tom Mix in those days: Jack Holden. He was also the announcer on the *Barn Dance*. They hired George Gobel to play the guitar and sing the theme song with us. He was 16 years old, and he played a boy who was about 13 on the show. His character was Jimmy. And I sang the baritone, Jack Holden sang the lead, and George Gobel played the guitar and sang tenor. That was in 1938.

Mel   That is great. I was never aware of that.

H.P.   I was doing seven characters on the show.

Mel   One of them was the sheriff, right?

H.P.   Yes, Sheriff Mike Shaw.

Mel   I grew up listening to and loving *Tom Mix*. Well, Hal, if I may call you that...

H.P.   Yes, I hope I haven't run up a big bill on you.

Mel   Not at all. It's been a delight. An absolute delight to talk to you. I can't begin to tell you how big a fan I have been of you through the years.

H.P.   Oh, that's swell.

Mel   I want to thank you very much for your time.

H.P.   Thank you, Mel, and good luck.

Mel   Thank you so much. Be well. Bye bye.

Jim Jordan
Fibber McGee and Molly

Mel   I grew up listening to *Fibber McGee and Molly* every Tuesday evening. May I ask you how you developed the idea for the show?

J.J.   Well, it stemmed from another show that we had done. And that stemmed from another show that we had done, if that makes sense! These things just evolved. It took 10 years for that to happen.

We started on the air in 1925, when we were singers.

Mel   You and your wife?

J.J.   Yes, we didn't speak. Finally we started talking on radio, and then we started doing little gags, and so on. Everything just stemmed from that. Later on, around 1927 or '28, we did a little skit on a farm program called *Luke and Mirandy*. This guy Luke was a god-awful liar, and that had kind of a country tone to it.

Then, the next thing, in 1929, '30, or '31, I forget the year, we moved to another radio station. We hired a writer that we had met. His name was Don Quinn. He was a commercial artist. He had a shop which was closed up during the Depression. He liked to write, and we met him, and he started writing for us.

In 1931 we moved from the Chicago local radio station, WENR to WMAQ, because WENR was sold to NBC. We were playing

Jim Jordan and Harold Peary

theaters at the time, and NBC would not let us do our theater dates on the radio. So we moved to WMAQ. We worked on a farm program there with a man named Farmer Rust. We had worked with him at WENR also. Is this too long?

Mel   No, no, please go on.

J.J.   [Laughs] Okay. He had told us about an old man that had a store down near the University of Missouri. The students at the university used to go in there. And this old guy would never have what they wanted. He'd say, "Well, I'm just smack out of that, but I'll be getting it in."

So these kids hung a sign on the front of that store called The Smackout. So we took that and said we would have an excuse for Marian and Jim to sing. We would have Luke, we called him Luke Grey, we had him running the store called Smackout.

We'd stop there every day, and Marian and I would sing. We did that for four years and sold it to the Johnson's Wax Company.

Mel   What year did Johnson's Wax buy the show?

The cast of *Fibber McGee and Molly*

J.J.   They bought us in October of 1934. We went on the air in April of 1935. In the interim we had meetings with the Johnson representatives a couple times a week. We didn't know what to call the show. We didn't know if we'd call it the Marian and Jim Jordan Show or something else.

It was suggested at the meeting one day by Don Quinn that we use the name Fibber McGee. Molly was a name that we used on other shows. That's how we got the name *Fibber McGee and Molly*!

Mel   How many years were you on the air?

J.J.   From 1925 til they found out what was the matter!

Mel   [Laughs] Early '50s, I think?

J.J.   No, we were on til 1960.

Mel   Wow, that is some run.

J.J.   The half-hour show ended in 1954. Then we went on *Monitor* after that. We did a 15-minute show five nights a week.

Mel   Fibber McGee and Molly were constantly at the top of the ratings. Other comedy shows always took a back seat to you. What are your fondest memories of the show as you think back?

J.J.   Pay day, I guess. I don't know. Nobody ever asked me that before! I don't know!

Mel   Thank you. Gee, it was a pleasure. You're just a delight to talk to. As a longtime fan of yours, I thank you immensely for your time.

J.J.   Thank you. Good-bye.

Parker Fennelly

Titus Moody on The Fred Allen Show

Mel   Mr. Fennelly, I have been a longtime admirer of yours. Not only with your many radio characters and your Pepperidge Farm commercials, which everybody knows and loves you for, but the thing I think everybody perhaps identifies Parker Fennelly with was the role of Titus Moody on *The Fred Allen Show*. May I ask you how it began, Mr. Fennelly, and how you actually developed that character?

P.F.   Well, Fred Allen was doing some special hour show, not his regular half-hour show. There was a character in it that I had played along the lines of Titus Moody. I think that probably led to Fred having me in the Alley. You see, I wasn't with Fred until long after he had been on the air with his program. I was with it three and a half seasons.

From that first appearance, he decided to write in a character along the lines of what I had on this other show, at which he was the MC. And that led to my being with him from then on. Some of the people who had been with him a long time were no longer with him when I was first with him.

Jack Smart and Teddy Bergman and some others had departed from the program, and I sort of filled in this character.

Parker Fennelly and Peter Donald

Mel   What year did you begin?

P.F.   I can't remember. Peter Donald will have to tell me. We started at
        the same time on Fred's show. It was the late '40s.

        I did a half season with Fred on television, which was abandoned
        because Fred was very uncomfortable in television.

Mel   I remember you on television, where they would use your voices and have puppets.

P.F.   That was true.

Mel   How was your role as Mr. Moody developed? Did you develop it yourself or did you develop it with writers?

P.F.   Well, I had been doing that kind of a role, that kind of a character, not so much exaggerated as Titus Moody, for many years. Fred, liking that New England character, wrote a good bit of the material, and it came about as Titus Moody. But I had been doing that kind of a character for many, many, many years.

Mel   Did you do that character on other radio programs?

P.F.   Yes, and in the theater to some extent.

Mel   I see. Are you a New Englander originally?

P.F.   I'm from Maine.

Mel   What part of Maine are you from?

P.F.   Northeast Harbor on Mount Desert Island, off the coast of Maine.

Mel   The thing I loved best about *The Fred Allen Show* was Allen's Alley. This was the most delightful part of the program. I thought you were on longer.

P.F.   Allen's Alley had been a part of the program before I joined, only different characters. Minerva had been with the show long before.

Mel Simons and the cast of Allen's Alley. From left to right –
Kenny Delmar (Senator Claghorn), Minerva Pious (Mrs. Nussbaum),
Mel Simons, Peter Donald (Ajax Cassidy), Parker Fennelly (Titus Moody).

Mel   So Minerva came before you joined the show?

P.F.   Oh, yes.

Mel   What was Fred Allen the personality like, as opposed to Fred
Allen the radio personality?

P.F.   He was a very nice person. He was very generous. I don't mean
about money, although that was true. He was generous about
everything. He was very thoughtful. He was always for the un-
derdog.

Mel   How about the famous Jack Benny/Fred Allen feud? They were
good buddies in real life, weren't they?

P.F.   Oh yeah, that was just made up. They were good friends.

Mel   How about Fred's ability to do adlib?

P.F.   Oh, yes. You see, in my mind, Benny was one of the greatest
          talents ever. His timing was so wonderful, and he could put things
          over. But I think as an ad-libber, Jack wouldn't have gone very
          far. But Fred was wonderful. His mind was like a steel trap.

Mel   I often got that impression. Did anything ever bother Fred?

P.F.   I told somebody yesterday that I don't think big problems both-
          ered Fred as much as some little things. For instance, we used to
          do the program on the third floor of the RCA Building. During
          the rehearsal, the door would be left unlocked. And sometimes
          tourists, going through the corridor, would open the door and
          look in at the actors rehearsing, and Fred would call out to them,
          it annoyed him very much, "How would you like it if we peeked
          at you?"

          Little things like that might have bothered him, but he was never
          disagreeable, at least to my knowledge.

Mel   Did anybody ever goof a line or fluff? I always had the impres-
          sion that he could just ride right over it and perhaps adlib his way
          out of it.

P.F.   I think he could, yes, I know he could.

Mel   You have been a wonderful interview, and I thank you very much.

Minerva Pious
Mrs. Nussbaum on
The Fred Allen Show

Mel   I am sitting here with one of my all-time favorite radio people, and I mean that sincerely. This is Minerva Pious, the very loveable Mrs. Nussbaum from *The Fred Allen Show*. My fondest memory of Minerva Pious is a gal who made me laugh every single week on *The Fred Allen Show*. I have always loved you!

M.P.   Thank you, Mel.

Mel   I would like to ask you how it all began with Fred Allen.

M.P.   I actually never had any background in show business. When I went with Fred Allen, I was an amateur, a parlor comic. A friend of mine by the name of Harry Tugend became Fred Allen's writer and got me a job, because I had a facility with dialects. I had a smattering of languages, and I was sold to Fred as the Ruth Draper of radio. Now, do you know what that means?

Mel   No.

M.P.   All right. Ruth Draper was the aunt of Paul Draper, the dancer. But Ruth Draper was an internationally known dialect expert. The only one in the world of this distinction. She wrote her own material, and when she performed in Italy, in the Italian lan-

Minerva Pious, Mel Simons, and Don Wilson

guage, the Italians stood up and cheered. The same thing happened in Germany, and in France, et cetera.

Now, Fred was only in his second year in radio, and he didn't know any radio actors and believed that I was the Ruth Draper of radio, you see. So he gave me a French part, I was a French lion tamer. I was also a Russian Countess that same day.

Now, I did those two parts. That night, the writer who had got me the job was pretty nervous about me. He said to Fred, "How did you like the new girl?"

And Fred said, "I could practically smell that lion cage."

Now, a week later I was home, thinking of my past glory, when the phone rang. A voice said, "Where are you?" They'd neglected to tell me it was a steady job. Which it was from 1933 until 1952. From 1933 to '49 on radio and the rest of the time on television.

Mel   I remember, *The Colgate Comedy Hour.*

M.P.   Right. And then in the next year, we, the whole company, did appearances on other television shows. In those days George Abbott, for example, had a *Goodrich Television Show*. And he put us all on, etcetera, etcetera.

Mel   As part of Allen's Alley?

M.P.   You keep saying Allen's Alley. Now let me clear that up. Allen's Alley was only five minutes of a half-hour show. And because people identified those four characters with that show, they did not know that the rest of it was a much better show than Allen's Alley. It was not, it was *The Fred Allen Radio Program*.

Mel   Right, I'm speaking about the specific part of the show where he would walk through Allen's Alley.

M.P.   Yes, but that's only five minutes of a show, and yet you keep calling the show Allen's Alley.

Mel   No, no, no. I wasn't calling the show Allen's Alley. I was referring to your part with Parker and the other gentlemen. But I think most people when they think back to *The Fred Allen Show*, this is what they remember.

M.P.   That's what you say! That's what you say!

Mel   You disagree with me?

M.P.   I disagree with you, because I still get letters saying, "I'll never forget you as the English Duchess, the Italian Countess." You see, you're too young to know anything but the Allen's Alley.

Mel   I caught the tail end of radio, and I remember Fred Allen. I loved it every week.

M.P.   Of course.

Mel   But the Allen's Alley segment, particularly you, Minerva, was the best.

M.P.   Well, thank you, but never mind about that.

Mel   Can I ask you about your personal association with Fred Allen?

M.P.   I remember the first day, about my French role, I said to him, "May I transpose a few sentences in that French line?"

And he was very, very courteous and respectful. He said, "No, I don't know French." I asked him a second time, and he said, "Yes, of course." And like an amateur, I overdid it. And when I went to him a third time, he said, "That'll be all right," and as I was walking away he said, "By the way, about the handwriting on the wall, what would you like to do about that?" [Laughs.]

Now, throughout the years, I think that I was the one who was least afraid of him. I was not afraid of him. You see, he had a dual personality. But I appreciated him to such an extent that I was never afraid of him. I couldn't understand why other people were. Now other actors on the program would say, "Gee, when does Fred tell you you're doing all right?" and so on.

And I said, "When did you ever have a boss who never opened his mouth to correct you or to direct you?" I said, "This is a star of such eminence, and he doesn't dare to tell you how to do it. If that isn't being a pat on the back, I don't know what is."

Now they were ashamed of themselves. Charles Laughton was a guest on the program. He said, "Where can we get a drink?" about a half hour before going on the air because I knew him and he had only just met Fred.

He had two quick drinks, and I said, "You're agitated. What is it all about?" He said, "How do you know when you're doing all right with Fred?"

So I said, "I'll tell you. I've been with him for 14 years, and I still don't know. But I somehow land on the program every week."

Then I said to him, "Do you think that Fred would presume to tell you how to do it, or to tell you whether you're good or bad?" Laughton was ashamed of himself. He just wanted to be patted on the back!

It's marvelous when you get into relationships of stars like that. Now when we were out on the West Coast once, Bing Crosby, who I knew also and Fred didn't at this time, he said, "Will you introduce me to Fred?"

I said, "What! You are both working on the same network. Do you mean to say you wouldn't walk into our studio and introduce yourself to Fred?"

He said, "No, because I revere him too much."

Mel   The thing that amazed me about Fred was his ability to adlib. Some of the shtick he did was just right off the top of his head!

M.P.   Well, you call it an ability to adlib. I call it a nimble brain and a wit. And how many people have that? Oh, once I was his wife, as a farmer's wife. We were all complaining because he wasn't giving us enough to eat. In the middle of this sketch, I got a frog in my throat. I cleared it, it came back. I cleared it again. It came back. He said, "You're always complaining about not enough to eat and concealing a frog in your throat!" [Laughs.]

Mel   How about the Benny-Allen feud? That was kind of a fun thing, wasn't it?

M.P.   Well, of course it was. I don't remember whether it was Jack or Fred that had a 10-year-old prodigy, a violin prodigy. It started that way. Fred said, "A 10-year-old kid can play better than you can." And that's how that feud started. Naturally it was a good-natured one. People were so enthralled with it. They really thought it was a real feud, etcetera, etcetera.

Mel   Let me ask you one last question, Minerva. Any special fond memories of being on *The Fred Allen Show*?

M.P.   Every week was a fond memory. Every week was a fresh script. Every week was topical. That's where Fred Allen differed from every other comedian. He read 35 periodicals a week to prepare for that program. He worked seven days a week. Now those periodicals didn't just come from the United States. They came from Great Britain, New Zealand, Australia, and the English-speaking countries. And that's why the program was so good. It didn't just come out of a joke book.

Mel   It was a lovely program.

M.P.   That's right.

Mel   And you are a lovely person.

M.P.   Thank you, Mel.

Mel   And I thank you. You're a doll.

M.P.   And so are you.

Mel   Thank you.

Kenny Delmar

Senator Claghorn on
The Fred Allen Show

Mel   I am with the one and only Mr. Kenny Delmar.

K.D.   Well, I've got to correct that a little bit. There is another Kenny Delmar. [Laughs.] He's my legitimate son. He will not use "junior." So I keep getting all his bills! Because he will not be junior. But otherwise, he's pretty good. He's got a very fine office where he makes motion pictures. How does it happen that I'm doing a commercial?

Mel   I don't even know what the question was, Ken.

K.P.   Well, I'm trying to sell my son without him even asking. I know both my sons well, because I'm related to them by marriage! [Laughs.]

Mel   Wonderful, wonderful. Anyway, I want to talk about Kenny Delmar, the performer. When I hear the name Kenny Delmar, immediately I think of Senator Claghorn.

K.D.   You do, huh? [Laughs.]

Mel   I do, Kenny, and so do many, many millions of others. I want to ask you how you got started with Fred Allen. How did it all begin, and what did you do prior to that. Did you do radio?

Kenny Delmar as Senator Claghorn

K.D.   Well, in radio, the Southern character of Senator Claghorn came from a hitchhike trip that I made to avoid a very beautiful French girl who wanted me to marry her.

So I went to California, and on the way I met this very nice Texan. He spoke with a very heavy Southern accent. He tried to talk over the sound of this loud truck. Instead of just talking, he yelled! That's how I got the idea.

I went to California, where I did this character for everybody, and they all seemed to like him. Then I came back to New York. I called this character Dynamite Gus.

I did this character for Orson Welles, because he was one of the people that we all worked with years ago on *The March of Time* and *Cavalcade*. Orson was doing a show called *Around the World in Eighty Days*. The character that he used, that I was supposed to do, he played, and he called him my name, Dynamite Gus. That was the name of the character.

When Fred Allen heard this character, he called me and made me a Southern senator. He made him Senator Claghorn. From that night, the first night I did it on the air, no one had heard him before on the air, I became Senator Claghorn. Fred Allen wrote my material.

Mel   Fred wrote all of your material?

K.D.   Yes. Fred wrote all of the material for Senator Claghorn. From that time on, I was a senator.

Mel   What years were you with Fred?

K.D.   I wasn't with him from the very beginning. There were others that were with Fred when he did *Town Hall Tonight*. I was with Fred for three years.

Mel   It's that funny. I thought it was longer!

K.D.   No, it seemed longer. What is really amazing, when you stop to consider, is how America responded happily for me. I was never on the air more than one minute and 15 seconds. In one week, America adopted this guy. Can you imagine? Being a success for one minute and 15 seconds?

Kenny Delmar and Mel Simons

Mel   You were also the announcer on the show, weren't you?

K.D.   I was the announcer. What I said was if the audience doesn't know me, I should be an announcer, because you get to say your name. So then the audience knew me as well as the agencies. That was the reason for that.

Mel   Did you do any other radio shows in addition to *Fred Allen*?

K.D.   Oh, I sure did. I did *Gang Busters*, I did *Columbia Workshop*; I did *The March of Time*.

Mel   Did you do these shows as a character actor?

K.D.   Oh, yes. A couple of times when Westbrook Van Voorhis was not available, I hosted *The March of Time*.

Mel   Tell me about Fred Allen the person.

K.D.   Well, every show with Fred Allen was memorable. He was a gentleman, number one. He was a very easy person to work with. He was a completely organized human being. We worked with Bob Hope, and you wouldn't believe the difference between the two shows.

Fred Allen had everything organized so well that there was never anybody who had to raise their voice, even to get the show rehearsed. I worked with Orson Welles.

Mel   On *War of the Worlds?*

K.D.   Yes, I played three parts on *War of the Worlds.* The show scared a lot of people. People were screaming at us. We had to answer the phone. I have never been sworn at, as on this occasion. It was a frightening experience.

Mel   Kenny, you've had a great career. I want to thank you very much. It has been an absolute delight to talk to you.

K.D.   Well, I certainly appreciate that. Thank you very much. You're a doll, Mel.

Peter Donald
Ajax Cassidy on The Fred Allen Show, Can You Top This

Mel   Peter, when did you begin on *The Fred Allen Show*?

P.D.   I suppose it was sometime around '47 or '48. It was the late '40s.

Mel   How did your character develop with Allen's Alley?

P.D.   Well, I had done 12 or 14 shows with my own show, *Can You Top This*. I had created sort of a cast of stock company characters. One being a little Irishman, whom I called Patty Mulvaney. Fred, in listening to *Can You Top This*, fell in love with the little Irishman. He called me up one day, and I went to our mutual agent. We had a meeting, and he said, "Will you do the little character?"

Fred had a great feeling for paradox. So Ajax Cassidy is just what you wouldn't call a child, anymore than you'd call your child Cassius Clay, I suppose. First he was going to call him Drum Gould, because he knew an Irish priest named Father Drum Gould. He rather liked the musical sound. So I was almost Ajax Drumgould. Cassidy, however, sounded more friendly. The character was my own. Everybody said, "Oh, you're doing Barry Fitzgerald." Well I was doing it over here, years before his second papers were dry. Before he even got his first papers from Irish Equity. The character is my own.

Mel   How would you describe Fred Allen as a person?

P.D.   He was very considerate. He was a big man. He had the funny eye on the world. He was not bitter about anything. He saw the gaiety in life. He was a very generous man. He was not particularly generous with himself. He was a little stingy with his own welfare. If it were raining cats and dogs, he would look for the old rubbers, rather than take a cab.

He was a little stingy with himself, I think. But as far as being wholeheartedly a good man, he was just that.

I had several happy years on the rewrite staff. I did that for nothing, just for the joy of working with him. So I got very close to him on the writing end of it. And that was a joy to work. That was just fun.

Mel   Tell us about Fred's feud with Jack Benny.

P.D.   I recall one time when they were nose to nose. Jack was on Fred's show, and of course, that we just involved in the feud thing. They actually loved each other. Fred stopped Jack cold, and Jack said, with his usual patsy kind of tone, "I'd give a thousand dollars to have an answer for that." And Fred said, "I'll sell you a half of one for five hundred!"

Mel   Do you remember any special incidents about Fred's adlibbing?

P.D.   I don't remember any particular incident. I do recall, though, that Fred was not thrown by anything. I think, particularly, Parker and I could break him up a little on the air.

Parker was a devilish man and a very funny man. Parker is one of the funniest gentlemen I know. Truly funny, that Mr. Fennelly is. We would sometimes deviate from the script a little bit. The audience was none the wiser, but we would break Fred up and then he'd come back and break us up. It was quite a party!

Mel   And this was on the air, not at rehearsal?

P.D.   Yes, oh this was on the air. We never got far enough from the script to lose it. That kind of fun in the studio is unprofessional. You may blow the whole thing. But I think Parker and I could just tease him a little bit, and you'd see him start to crack up on the air. Those were funny times, I think.

Mel   Peter, I want to ask you something else. Outside of *The Fred Allen Show*, you're one of the finest storytellers I've ever heard. I loved your stories on *Can You Top This*. Your stories were sensational. I'd like you to talk a little bit about the program *Can You Top This* and how you started, and the number of years you were associated with it.

P.D.   Well, I had been a radio actor. I was a serious radio actor. I played opposite Helen Hayes, Maude Adams, Ethel Barrymore, Gertrude Lawrence, and the like. Here's something that only occurred to me now. I used to be radio understudy for Parker Fennelly. When I was only 18 or 19 years of age, on a CBS show called *Wilderness Road*, Parker played an old New England preacher. When he went on vacation, I filled in for him. I did the role with a New England dialect. I became Parker number two. We hadn't really met at that time. Years later we became neighbors on the Alley.

Mel   What was it like working on *Can You Top This*? I had the pleasure of meeting Harry Hershfield a few years ago. I had never met Senator Ford or Joe Laurie Jr. What were they like?

P.D.   Well, they were very, very different. Joe Laurie was the peppery little vaudevillian, the tough little monkey from Hell's Kitchen, New York. Senator Ford was from Long Island. He was kind of a deadpan sour-pussed fellow, and Harry, of course, was forever youthful. Harry was 89 when he passed on a few months ago. Harry actually got around more than any of us. He was a wonderful toastmaster. He usually had the latest jokes or updated them.

It was a party. For many years we were on twice a week. We did a local show on Wednesday, plus the network show on Saturday. We were on the air for 16 years.

We didn't socialize. We didn't go to each other's homes much. We were all members of the Lamb's Club, so there was an affinity there. We got along very well. It was a game every time. It was just like a good party. We looked forward to the broadcast.

Mel   And there was no rehearsal on their part?

P.D.   No.

Mel   They did not know the subject matter?

P.D.   No. I had my own dressing room, and I was practically smuggled in the side door. The general manager of the show would come in with the four jokes of the week, which he picked out of several hundred, and give them to me. Then I would rewrite them and do a little monologue, a little play out of it.

The boys never knew the subject matter. See, the trick was this: They did have a vast collection of jokes. But they twisted anything. They could use a key word and twist it around.

Mel   I always got a kick out of Hershfield particularly.

P.D.   Oh, he was marvelous.

Mel   He very rarely got under a thousand on the laugh meter.

P.D.   Well, we were all paid very well. There was no prize for best in class or anything like that. But one time we did a kind of a survey on who topped whom the most, and it came out about even.

Mel   Was Senator Ford the originator of the show?

P.D.   Yes, he thought up the whole thing.

Mel   Now you mentioned 16 years. From when to when?

P.D.   Prior to World War II, a year or two before Pearl Harbor to the mid-'50s.

Mel   Then they tried the show on television, but not with the same impact.

P.D.   On TV they did it cheaply and wrong. They weren't paying the people enough, and they were paying only the people who wanted to do it. On TV, not all of the comedians were storytellers, and not all storytellers were good storytellers. Those were the elements missing, and that's why the show, I think, fell apart.

Mel   Thank you for a great interview.

Freeman Gosden
Amos on Amos 'n' Andy

F.G.   Hello!

Mel   Hello, Freeman Gosden?

F.G.   Yes.

Mel   It's a thrill to talk to you, sir. My name is Mel Simons, and I'm calling from Boston, Massachusetts. I'm a longtime admirer and fan of yours and of *Amos 'n' Andy*.

F.G.   Yes.

Mel   I'm writing a book on old-time radio.

F.G.   There are about four guys I know who are doing the same thing.

Mel   Yes, so I hear, but frankly you just can't write a book about radio without including Freeman Gosden and Charles Correll.

F.G.   That's very flattering of you, but here is the thing. We quit the business, I got out of the business, let's put it that way. We would like to leave it clean and would not like to get into it and tell a lot of stories about our experiences and why we left....

The cast of Amos 'N' Andy radio show – (left to right) Lou Lubin, Madaline Lee, Charles Correll (Andy), Ruby Dandridge, one of the Jubalaires, Freeman Gosden (Amos), and Eddie Green. In the background are the Jubalaires.

Mel   Oh, no, no. Let me assure you, this is strictly entertainment, I would not get into any controversy or ask you anything embarrassing in the least.

F.G.   What type of stuff do you want to write?

Mel   I just want to ask you how you got the idea for it, the years that you were on, how you developed your characters.

F.G.   I tell you what. That has been printed a thousand times. Really it has, and I don't think we have ever had an interview that the first question wasn't, how did you get started in this business, what inspired you to do it? How did you create the characters? That has been done a thousand times. Honestly it has, and I just think it is a waste of your time and mine, and your money on long distance, to try and go over some of this stuff again. To tell you the truth, I just slipped so much of it from my mind, I don't remember half of it now. My partner is dead, as you know.

Mel   Yes, I know. He passed away a couple of years ago, I believe.

F.G.   Yeah.

Mel   Well, can I ask you just a few simple questions? I'd like to ask you the years that you were on. How many years you were on, and the year that you started.

F.G.   God, I'd have to go in and get the books out and find out. I pay no more attention to dates than the man in the moon! Truthfully, I don't!

Mel   Well, how many years all together were you on radio?

F.G.   I don't remember that exactly.

Mel   I see... Well, I thank you very much for your time, Mr. Gosden...

F.G.   Well, I'm sorry that I can't be of help to you, but truthfully I've had about six of these lately, and I didn't do anything about them. I think it would be unfair, especially to the one fellow that I know, that shall be nameless, but he said as a personal favor would you do it, and I didn't get into it there. I just don't want to start it now.

Freeman Gosden and Charles Correll

Mel   I understand.

F.G.   And I'm sorry as hell, and I hope you'll understand.

Mel   No, I respect your feelings. I understand perfectly, and it was just a thrill to talk to you, Mr. Gosden.

F.G.   Well, thank you.

Mel   I thank you for your time.

F.G.   You're welcome.

Mel   Thank you. Bye bye.

Printed in the United States
80456LV00005BA/106-153